Test Automation using Microsoft Coded UI with C#

Navneesh Garg

Vaibhav Mittal

- Microsoft Visual Studio 2015

- Learn Automation on a Web Based Application

- Real Life Experiences

- Step By Step Instructions

- Interview Questions Based on Microsoft Coded UI

Microsoft Coded UI Step By Step Guide

Test Automation Using Microsoft Coded UI with C#

Navneesh Garg
Vaibhav Mittal

ISBN - 978-0-9922935-4-3

Publisher: Adactin Group Pty Ltd.

Contents

About the Authors

Navneesh Garg

Navneesh Garg is a recognized test automation architect and corporate trainer, specializing in test automation, performance testing, security testing and test management. As a tool specialist, he has worked on a variety of functional automation tools including Microsoft CodedUI, Selenium, HP QTP/UFT, TestComplete, TestPartner, SilkTest, Watir, RFT, and on varied technologies including Web, Java, .NET, SAP, Peoplesoft and Seibel.

His previous books "Test Automation using Unified Functional Testing" and "Test Automation using Selenium WebDriver" are among best - selling books on test automation. These books have consistently ranked among the top 100 testing books on Amazon.

He is an entrepreneur and founder of several successful IT companies which encompass the Adactin Group, CresTech Software, and Planios Technologies.

As an experienced corporate trainer, he has trained professionals in Microsoft CodedUI, Selenium and other test tools across a wide range of global clients such as Macquarie Bank, Corporate Express, Max New York Life, Accenture, NSW Road and Maritime Services, Australian Dept of Education, HCL Technologies, Sapient, Fidelity Group, Adobe Systems, and many more. He has training experience in diverse geographies such as Australia, India, Hong Kong and USA.

As a technical test delivery head for his company, he has led and managed functional automation testing and performance testing teams across a wide range of domains, using commercial tools and open source tools. Certified in HP QTP, HP Quality Center, HP LoadRunner, IBM Rational Functional Tester and as a Certified Ethical Hacker, he has designed several high-end automation frameworks including using Selenium and its integrations with tools like TestNG, JUnit, Selenium Grid, Jenkins and ANT.

Vaibhav Mittal

Vaibhav Mittal is a seasoned consultant with a vast experience in Information and Technology. He has experience working on many projects in software development and testing, exposed to multiple technologies including Microsoft .NET, Java, Oracle, ETL, Business Intelligence and Analytics. His professional journey enabled him to work across different geographies like USA, Europe, Japan and India with many esteemed organisations like Adobe Systems, Oracle, Procter & Gamble, Pfizer and Novartis.

Vaibhav is Delivery Head with Adactin Group Pty. Ltd, Sydney. During his stint with Adactin, Vaibhav has worked on various projects in Agile and other project management methodologies. He is not only an experienced project manager but a tool expert in testing. His wide knowledge in tools include Microsoft Coded UI, Selenium, UFT, QC/ALM and many more.

Vaibhav, as a corporate trainer, prepares and delivers courses on various technologies helping many professionals elevate their IT skills. He has presented papers at international forums, which makes him a thorough and a passionate IT professional.

Preface

Our motivation for writing this book stems from our hands-on experience in the IT and testing domains and the experience we have gained as automation consultants working in numerous complex automation projects.

Coded UI, being an automation tool from Microsoft, is gaining huge popularity but still is not perceived as an easy to use tool especially by testers due to a variety of reasons, including tool setup, programming background and support issues. A key objective of this book is to showcase in a simple guided way how to use Microsoft Coded UI so that you can attain maximum return on investment from using the tool. Not only will you learn how to use the tool but also how to effectively create maintainable frameworks using Coded UI.

Scope of Topics

As part of the scope of this book we will cover **Microsoft Coded UI with C#** as the programming language with Visual Studio 2015.

We will be using **Visual Studio 2015**as the main IDE for creating Coded UI tests.

No prior knowledge of C# language is required for this book but having an understanding of object oriented programming language concepts will definitely help. As part of this book we will be covering **Basics of C#** which would be required to use **Microsoft Coded UI** for beginner users.

We will also learn how Microsoft Coded UI integrates with **continuous Integration** tools like **Team Foundation Server.**

Ourintent in this book is to discuss the key features of Microsoft Coded UI and cover all crucial aspects of the tool in order to help you **create effective automation frameworks using Microsoft Coded UI**.

TargetAudience

The target audience for this book are manual, functional testers who want to **learn Microsoft Coded UI quickl**y and who want to create effective automation frameworks that generate positive ROIs to stakeholders.

Salient Features of this Book

This book has been designed with the objective of **simplicity and ease of understanding**.

A major fear amongst functional testers who want to learn Coded UI is the fear of the programming language and coding. We address these fears by covering just enough **basics on C# programming language** that will give you the confidence to use Microsoft Coded UI.

This book follows a **unique training based approach** instead of a regular text book approach. Using a step by step approach, weguide you through the exercises using pictorial snapshots.

We also provide step by step installation and configuration of Visual Studio before using Coded UI.

Instead of using custom html pages with few form fields and links, this book utilizes a custom developed, Web based application containing many form fields and links.

Another differentiator is that wehave tried to include **many practical examples and issues** which most automation testers encounter in their day-to-day activities. We share our real-life experience with you to give you an insight into what challenges you could face while implementing an automation solution on your project. Our practical examples cover how to use most of the features within Microsoft Coded UI.

We also cover aspects of **Continuous Integration tool; Team Foundation Server** so that Coded UI scripts can be integrated with the development environment and run on nightly builds.

Finally, the book includes a special section devoted to answering the most **common interview questions** relating to test automation and Microsoft Coded UI.

Sample Application and Source Used in Book

The sample application used in the book can be accessed at the following URL:

www.adactin.com/HotelApp/

The source code used in the book can be found at the following link

www.adactin.com/store/

Feedback and Queries

For any feedback or queries you can contact the author at www.adactin.com/contact.html or email navneesh.garg@adactin.com or vaibhav.mittal@adactin.com

Order this book

For bulk orders, contact us at orders@adactin.com

You can also place your order online at adactin.com/store/

Acknowledgements

I would like to thank my family (my parents, my wife Sapna, my wonderful kids Shaurya and Adaa) for their continued support. Without them this book would not have been possible.

I would also like to thank my colleagues and clients for the inspiration, knowledge and learning opportunities provided.

Navneesh Garg

I would like to thank my family (my parents, my wife Sangeeta, my lovely boy Vedaang) who supported and encouraged me in spite of all the time it took me away from them. Without them this book would not have been possible.

I would like to express my gratitude to the many people who saw me through this book; to all those who provided support, talked things over, read, wrote, offered comments, allowed me to quote their remarks and assisted in the editing, proofreading and design.

Vaibhav Mittal

Special thanks to William B for his review and feedback, which immensely helped as we worked on this book.

৩

1.

Introduction to Automation

Introduction

In this chapter we will talk about automation fundamentals and understand what automation is and the need for automation. An important objective of this chapter is to understand the economics of automation, and determine when we should carry out automation in our projects. We will also discuss some popular commercial and open source automation tools available in the market.

Key objectives:

- What is automation?
- Why automate? What are the benefits of automation?
- Economics of automation
- Commercial and Open Source automation tools

1.1 What is Functional Automation?

Automation testing is to automate the execution of manually designed test cases without any human intervention.

The purpose of automated testing is to execute manual functional tests quickly and in a cost-effective manner. Frequently, we re-run tests that have been previously executed (also called regression testing) to validate functional correctness of the application. Think of a scenario where you need to validate the username and password for an application which has more than 10,000 users. It can be a tedious and monotonous task for a manual tester and this is where the real benefits of automation can be harnessed. We might need to free up a manual functional tester's time so that they can perform other key tasks while automation provides extensive coverage to the overall test effort.

When we use the term "automation", there is usually a confusion about whether automation scope includes functional and performance testing or not Automation covers both.

- Functional Automation – Used for automation of functional test cases in the regression test bed.

- Performance Automation – Used for automation of non-functional performance test cases. An example of this is measuring the response time of the application under considerable (for example 100 users) load.

Functional automation and performance automation are two distinct terms and their automation internals work using different driving concepts. Hence, there are separate tools for functional automation and performance automation.

For the scope of this book, we will be only referring to **Functional Automation**.

1.2 Why do we Automate?

Find below key benefits of Functional Automation:

1. Effective Smoke (or Build Verification) Testing

Whenever a new software build or release is received, a test (generally referred to as "smoke test" or "shakedown test") is run to verify if the build is testable for a bigger testing effort and major application functionalities are working correctly. Many times we spend hours doing this only to discover that a faulty software build resulted in all the testing efforts going towaste. Testing has to now start all over again after the release of a new build.

If the smoke test is automated, then the smoke test scripts can be run by the developers to verify the build quality before releasing the code to the testing team.

2. Standalone - Lights Out Testing

Automated testing tools can be programmed to kick off a script at a specific time.

If needed, automated tests can be automatically kicked off overnight, and the testers can analyze the results of the automated test the next morning. This will save valuable test execution time for the testers.

3. Increased Repeatability

At times it becomes impossible to reproduce a defect which was found during manual testing. A likely reason for this could be that the tester forgot which combination of test steps led to the error message; hence, he is unable to reproduce the defect. Automated testing scripts take the guess work out of test repeatability.

4. Testers can Focus on Advanced Issues

As tests are automated, automated scripts can be base-lined and re-run for regression testing. Regression tests generally yield fewer new defects as opposed to testing newly developed features. So, functional testers can focus on analyzing and testing newer or more complex areas that have the potential for most of the defects while automated test scripts can be used for regression test execution.

5. Higher Functional Test Coverage

With automated testing a large number of data combinations can be tested which may not be feasible with manual testing. We use the term 'Data driven testing' which means validating numerous test data combinations using one automated script.

6. Other Benefits

- **Reliable:** Tests perform precisely the same operations each time they are run, thereby eliminating human error.
- **Repeatable:** You can test how the software reacts under repeated execution of the same operations.
- **Programmable:** You can program sophisticated tests that bring out hidden information from the application.
- **Comprehensive:** You can build a suite of tests that cover every feature in your application.
- **Reusable:** You can re-use tests on different versions of an application, even if the user-interface changes.
- **Better Quality Software:** Because you can run more tests in less time with fewer resources.
- **Fast:** Automated tools run tests significantly faster than human users.

1.3 When should we Automate? Economics of Automation

Let us take a scenario. If your Test Manager asks you whether it is advisable for your company to automate an application or not, how would you respond?

In this scenario, the manager is interested in knowing if functional automation will deliver the organization a better return on investment (ROI) besides improving application quality and test coverage.

We can determine whether we should automate a given test if we can determine that the cost of automation would be less than the total cost of manually executing the test cases.

For example, if a test script is to run every week for the next two years, automate the test if the cost of automation is less than the cost of manually executing the test 104 times (2 years will have 104 weeks).

Calculating the **Cost of Test Automation**

Cost of Automation = Cost of tool + labor cost of script creation + labor cost of script maintenance

Automate if:

Cost of automation is lower than the manual execution of those scripts.

The key idea here is to plan for the cost of script maintenance. We have seen a lot of automation projects fail because project managers did not plan for the labor costs involved in script maintenance.

Example

Let us give you an example from our personal experience.

We performed some automation work for one of our investment banking clients. We had a five-member team, which automated almost 3000 test cases in about six months time, which included around 30 total man months of effort. At the end of project, we gave the client's testing team, a hand-over of the entire automation suite created by our team. Our recommendation to them was that they would need at least a one or two member team to continuously maintain the scripts. This was because there were still functional changes happening to the application and scripts would need maintenance. But since the client project manager had no budget allocated for this activity, they over looked this advice and continued to execute automation scripts. After the first six months of the 3000 test cases, only 2000 test cases passed, while the rest started failing. These scripts failures were because script fixes were needed due to application changes. The client team was okay with that and continued to execute those 2000 working test cases, and got rid of the remaining 1000 test cases, which were now executed manually. After another six months, only scripts corresponding to 1000 test cases passed. So they got rid of another 1000 test cases and started executing them manually. After another six months (1.5 years in total), all the Scripts failed and testing had to move back to manual functional testing.

In the above real-life scenario, the cost of automation and its benefits could have been reaped, if the client had allocated 1-2 automation testers (could have been part-time) to maintain the scripts and had properly planned and budgeted for it.

1.4 Commercial and Open Source Automation Tools

This section lists some of the popular Commercial and Open Source Automation Tools.

Vendor	Tool	Details
OpenSource (free)	Selenium	Open Source tool and market leader in Open Source segment. Primarily for Web-based automation. Supports C#, Java, Python, and Ruby programming languages.

OpenSource (free)	Watir	Watir stands for "Web application testing in Ruby". It is again primarily for Web application automation and uses Ruby as the programming language.
Microsoft	VSTP – Code UI tests	Code UI tests come with Microsoft Visual studio Enterprise version. You can program using VB.net or C# as languages of choice. Fairly good for technical testers.
HP	Unified Functional Testing	HP UFT (previous version was called QTP) is the market leader in Test Automation in the commercial tools segment. It uses VBScript as the programming language and its ease of use makes it a tool of choice against other competing tools.
IBM	Rational Functional Tester	IBM Rational Functional tester is another popular test Automation Tool. We can program in VB.net or Java using this tool. Is recommended for technical testers.
Microfocus	SilkTest	Microfocus bought SilkTest from Borland. It is still a very popular automation tool which uses 4Test (propriety) language. Good for technical testers.
SmartBear	TestComplete	Low cost alternative to other commercial tools with good automation features. Supports VBScript, JScript, C++Script, C#Script and DelphiScript languages.

❧

2.

Training Application Walkthrough

In this chapter we will introduce our customized Web based training application, which we will use as a part of our book.

Key Objectives

1. Training application walkthrough
2. Understand a sample scenario.

2.1 Training Application Walkthrough

A single, custom, Web based application will be used throughout this book. We are using this Web based application because this book's focus is onMicrosoft's Coded UI automation tool which supports Web based applications. Also 80-90% of applications tested and automated in real projects are Web based applications. Our training application will therefore provide you with a very good example of a realistic application on which to learn how to automate a Web based application.

Our sample application is a simple hotel booking web application, which has the following key features

- Search for a Hotel
- Book a Hotel
- View Booked Itinerary
- Cancel Booking

Let us browse through the application

1. Launch IE and enter URL *www.adactin.com/HotelApp* to see Login page.

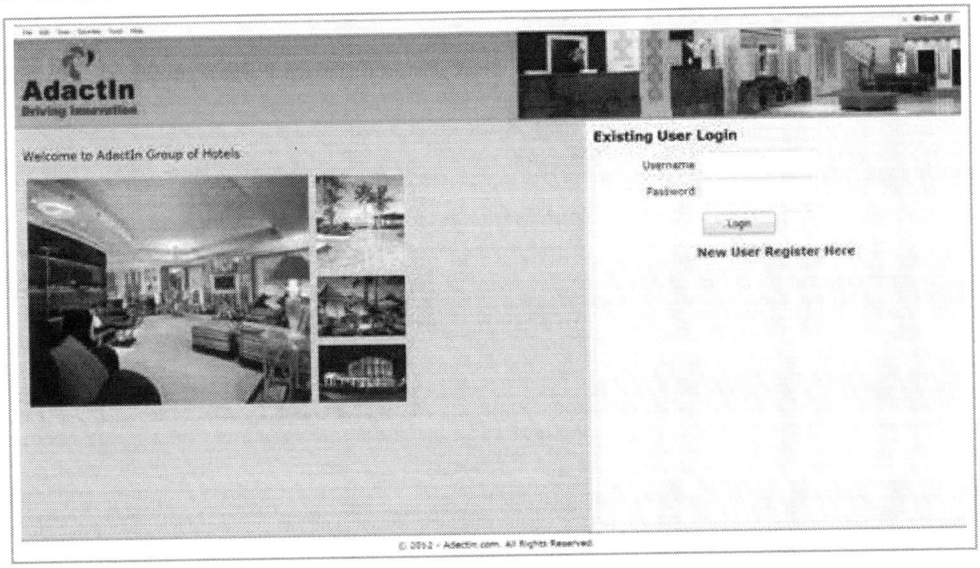

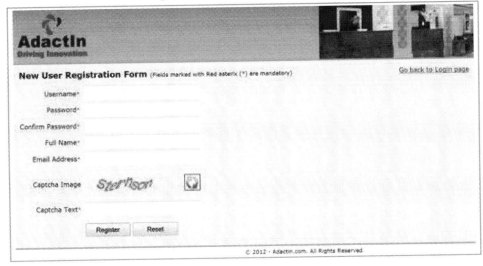

Figure 2-1 – Application Login Page

2. Click on "**New User Register Here**" to go to the Registration page.

Figure 2-2 – Application Registration Page

3. Register yourself by entering all of the fields. Remember the username and password as you will be using this username/password to login to the application both manually and later via an automation script.

4. After you register, an automatic email will be sent to your email-id for confirmation. If you do not receive the email, then check your junk folder for the email.

5. Click on the confirmation link in the body of the email.

6. Go to the Login page link.

7. On the Login page use the username/password that you registered earlier, and click on the **Login** button. You will come to the Search Hotel Page.

8. Search for a Hotel-

    i. Select a location, e.g., Sydney

    ii. Select Number of Rooms e.g., 2

    iii. Select Adults per Room, e.g.2

    iv. Click the **Search** button

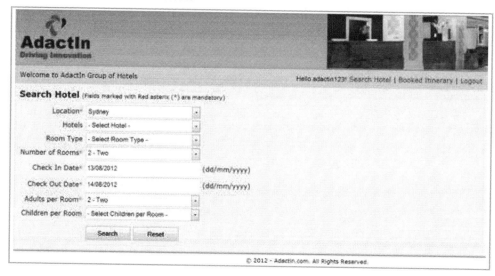

Figure 2-3 – Application Search Hotel Page

9. Select a Hotel-

    i. **Select** one of the Hotel Radio Buttons, e.g., select radio button next to Hotel Cornice

    ii. Click the Continue button

Figure 2-4 – Application Select Hotel Page

10. Book a Hotel-

    i.   Enter First Name

    ii.   Enter Last Name

    iii. Enter Billing Address

    iv. Enter 16-digit credit Card Number

    v.   Select Credit Card Type

    vi. Select Expiry Month

    vii. Select Expiry Year

    viii.Enter CVV Number

    ix. Click the **Book Now** button

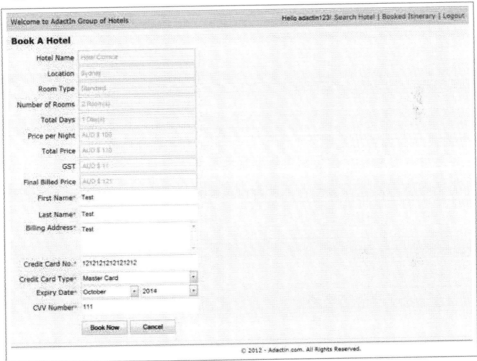

Figure 2-5 – Application Book a Hotel Page

11. When the Booking Confirmation page appears, you will notice that an Order No. is generated.

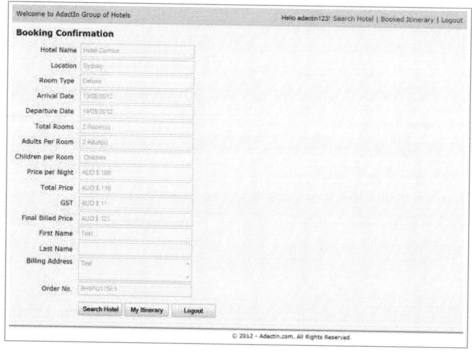

Figure 2-6 – Application Booking Confirmation Page

12. Copy the Order No. to the clipboard. In this case it is 8K1l446G95.

13. Click the **My Itinerary** Button or click the **Booking Itinerary** link at the top right corner of the page. The **Booked Itinerary** page should open.

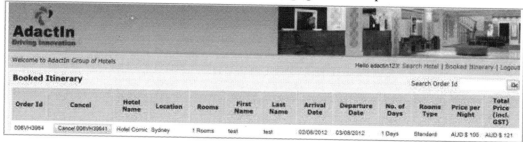

Figure 2-7 – Application Booked Itinerary Page

14. Enter the Order No. copied in the previous step in the Search Order Id field, and click the **Go** button. You will see the order you recently created...

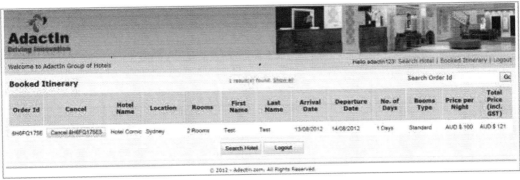

Figure 2-8 – Application Search Results Page

15. Click the **Logout** button or Logout link, on the top right corner to logout from the application. You will go to the "**Click here to login again**" page.

Figure 2-9 – Application Click here to login again Page

16. Click the"**Click here to login again**" link to go to the login page

> **Note:** Hotel Application has 2 builds:
>
> - Build 1 – Has been developed with known defects. Therefore, a few functional test cases and automation scripts will fail on this build.
> - Build 2 – Known defects have been fixed. Therefore, a few functional test cases and automation test scripts should pass when executed on this build

The user can access either of the builds from the Login page of the Hotel Application

3.

Planning before Automation

Introduction

Before you start recording your automation scripts, it is important to plan the recording of your scripts. You need to determine:

- Which test cases need to be automated.
- Each priority level and automate the test cases with the highest priority levels first.
- The stability of the application.
- The data dependency between the tests.
- If there are tests which use the same data.
- If the automation tester knows the steps of the tests to be automated.
- Whether or not the automation testers have permission to access the components of the application and the systems.
- Who is going to automate which test cases within the team.
- When the automation tasks should be completed.

In this chapter, we will try to understand what we need to plan before we start our recording.

Key objectives:

- To understand the pre-requisites before we record.
- To understand the Test Automation process.

3.1 Pre-requisites Before you Start Recording

Let us try to understand some of the pre-requisites before we start recording our scripts:

- Prepare your Test Environment - Check whether your environment and application are stable

Determine that you have a test environment available in which you can record/replay and create your automation scripts.

Determine whether the application is stable from a development as well as functional point of view. Does the interface change very often?

As a recommendation, if the application interface is changing too often, or if the application is not stable from a functional point of view, or if the test environment is not stable, we should not start automation. It's important to understand the factual reason for that. Technically speaking, we can still perform automation, but it might increase maintenance and script modification effort later on, when functional issues or UI issues are fixed. So a better approach is to wait until the environment is stable.

- Ensure that the automation tester has permission to access application components and systems

Ensure that the test suite and testers have permissions to access the database, host systems, and input/output data.

- Execute the test case steps manually to determine the expected results

Execute the test case steps manually on the application, to verify that all steps are listed and ensure that you are able to understand the business process. One of the most important factors to consider in automated testing is to ensure that the test describes the test steps in the most straight forward manner possible. It is important to **capture the actions** stated in the test case **exactly as an end-user would perform** them in the business process.

Also, it helps you to understand if there is any **pre-data setup** required for the test. For example, if you need to automate the login process, then you need to have a valid username and password. Rather than starting your recording first, you will realize that you need a valid login when you first manually execute your tests.

Example

Let us give you another example from our personal experience:

Once we were implementing functional automation for a client and We had a test case to verify the expiry of login after two months. We thought of changing the system date of our PC to two months in the past and then verifying the login expiry. But the question was: How do we change the system date using HP UFT? So we did some research and tried a couple of examples, and were able to figure out a way. But that took us about two days.

Now once we had implemented the solution, we found that whenever we ran the UFT script, the login did not actually expire and the user could still login. We ran the test case steps manually and found the login does not expire even when manually executed which got us perplexed. After some more investigations, we realised that we were changing the system date of our local PC and not the server. But as the expiry date was linked to the server date and not to the local machine, the login did not expire and the user could login. Also, we did not have access to the server, and due to authorization issues it was not possible to change the date of the server machine.

The question is: Could we have foreseen this issue and saved two days? If we would have manually tested this scenario, we would have realized our mistake and would not have spent two days trying to automate it.

- Determine what data will be required for test execution

Ensure that you understand what input data you will need for test creation. You need to understand valid and invalid input data. Also, a lot of times there are scenarios where you would need data in a specific format or type.

Example

Let us take an example here:

We used to work for a mortgage domain client. One of their applications required the input date to be greater than or equal to the current date. How do we design an automation script to take a date that's greater than the current date without the test case depending on the already defined data? It needs better planning. As a solution, instead of using hard-coded data, we used a VBScript function to generate a date greater than today's date.

Apart from this, there might be scenarios where after the test verification has finished; you would need to roll back specific data that was earlier setup as part of test execution. So make sure to understand data dependencies before you begin automating.

- Determine the start and end point of the test and follow it for all of your automation scripts

Make sure you determine where each of your automated scripts will start from and where they will end.

Why is this important? This is important as you are going to run your scripts as a suite or a batch and not individually. So your current script should know where your previous script ended.

For instance, say you are working on a Web based application and you open your browser at the start of every test but fail to close the browser at the end of each test. If you are running 50 tests, then you will have 50 browser windows open at the end of your script run which will cause script execution issues.

The correct way is to determine the Start and End point of your test and follow it for all of your scripts. This will ensure that any automation tester on your team will know which form or page of the application will be open when they start creating their automation script and where they should finish their script.

A better solution for Web based applications will be to open the browser at the start of every test and close the browser at the end of every test.

- Reset any master data, if data is modified as part of your test

Another important thing to do is to reset any master data to the default value, after data is modified as part of your test. The reason is that future test scripts would be looking for default data and not the data which you have modified as part of your current test.

Example

Let us give an example here:

We were once working on a manufacturing based application which had units (centimetres, millimetres, and inches) defined as master data to measure the length of various manufacturing components. As a part of one test case we automated, we changed the master data of the Unit field from centimetres to inches, and verified that all of the valid lengths were changed to inches. Our automation script worked beautifully, and we integrated it with our automation suite and executed our overnight test run.

The next morning we found that all of our scripts, following this script failed. We realized that though we had changed the master data of the Unit field from centimetres to inches, we never changed it back to the default (which was centimetres). Hence, all the sequential scripts failed as they expected the unit to be centimetres, but found the unit in inches. So we had to fix the script to reset the unit field back to the default value at the end of the script.

So as a thumb rule, reset all of the master data that you have modified at the end of your test to the default values as it can impact other tests.

- Standardize naming conventions

Create standards and conventions on how you are going to name your automation scripts, setup naming conventions for your temporary variables, functions, and other components of your automation framework.

This will help to ensure that the whole team is following standardized naming conventions and the complete framework can be easily maintained.

- Plan and prioritize your test cases. Identify your automation candidates

Plan and prioritize which test cases you should automate first. We use the term ***automation candidates*** for regression test cases, which we select for automation.

A few key criteria for selection of automation candidates include:

- Test cases which are high priority or linked to high priority requirements. Usually we automate Sanity or Build Acceptance test cases as a first step.
- Test cases which are data oriented or which need to be executed multiple times for different sets of data.
- Test cases which take a long time to execute and their automation will free up functional testers to perform more key tasks.

- Existing or fixed defects in the systems which are now converted to test cases.

- Frequency of execution of the test cases. Test cases which are executed very frequently are better candidates for automation giving more Return on Investment (ROI).

- Test cases for operating system compatibility or browser compatibility can be automated, as the same script can be executed for different operating systems or browsers.

- Plan resources and schedule

Plan how many people will be automating the test cases, and what will be the delivery schedule.

3.2 Test Automation Process

This section describes automation processes usually followed as we automate the regression test cases.

1. Defining the scope for automation: Define the scope of test cases that should be automated, check feasibility, and confirm return on investment.

2. Selection of the Test Automation tool: Select right test automation tools, which will suit your application technology and fit into your budget. It can be an open source or a commercial tool.

3. Procurement of licenses: If a commercial tool is selected, procure the license for the commercial tool.

4. Training the testers to use the tool: If required, train the testing team on how to perform automation and how to use the automation tool.

5. Automation strategy and plan: Design the automation strategy and plan on how and when regression test cases will be automated. Also, define data dependencies, environmental needs and risks.

6. Identification and development of Automation Framework and Test Automation Lab: An Automation framework is required to make sure automation scripts are maintainable. It involves setting up design and guidelines of automation components. This includes defining naming conventions, guideline document, structure of the automation scripts and setup of test machines in the test environment.

7. Creation of Automation Scripts: Actual recording or creation of automation scripts from regression test cases.

8. Peer Review and Testing: Review of Automation Scripts by peers to ensure that all conventions are followed and automation scripts are correctly mapped to functional test cases. Test case verification points are also verified as part of the review.

9. Integration of scripts: This involves integration of automation scripts into a larger automation suite for overnight test execution, in a batch process.

10. Script maintenance: Regular script maintenance that is required when an application undergoes functional changes and needs fixes in the automation scripts.

❧

4.

Introduction to Coded UI

Introducing Coded UI

Coded UI Test (CUIT) was introduced by Microsoft with Visual Studio 2010. Coded UI tests drive your automated tests through its user interface (UI). These tests include functional testing of the UI controls. They let you verify that the whole application, including its user interface, is functioning correctly. Coded UI Tests are particularly useful where there is validation or other logic in the user interface, for example in a web page. They are also frequently used to automate existing manual test.

Key objectives:

- Understand Coded UI Tests
- Coded UI Framework
- Supported Configurations and Platforms for Coded UI Tests
- Installation Requirements for Coded UI

4.1 Understand Coded UI Tests

A typical development experience might be one where, initially, you simply build your application (F5) and click-through the UI controls to verify that things are working correctly. You then might decide to create a coded test so that you don't need to continue to test the application manually. Depending on the particular functionality being tested in your application, you can write code for either a functional test or for an integration test that might or might not include testing at the UI level. If you simply want to directly access some business logic, you might code a unit test. However, under certain circumstances, it can be beneficial to include testing of the various UI controls in your application. A coded UI test can automate the initial (F5) scenario, verifying that code churn does not impact the functionality of your application.

This is illustrated in the image below -

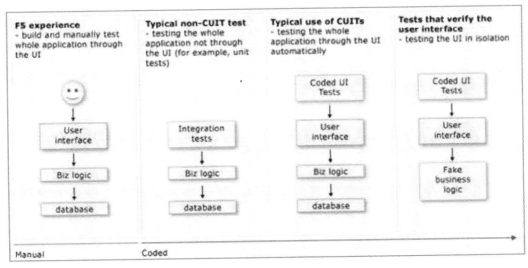

Figure 4.1 – Coded UI for Automation

Creating a coded UI test is easy. You simply perform the test manually while the CUIT Test Builder runs in the background. You can also specify what values should appear in specific fields. The CUIT Test Builder records your actions and generates code from them. After the test is created, you can edit it in a specialized editor that lets you modify the sequence of actions.

The specialized CUIT Test Builder and editor make it easy to create and edit coded UI tests even if your main skills are concentrated in testing rather than coding. But if you are a developer and you want to extend the test in a more advanced way, the code is structured so that it is straight forward to copy and adapt. For example, you might record a test to buy something from a website, and then edit the generated code to add a loop that buys many items.

> **Note:** The introduction to Coded UI is taken from MSDN (https://msdn.microsoft.com/en-us/library/dd286726.aspx#VerifyingCodeUsingCUIT Create). You can visit this page for more details.

4.2 Coded UI Framework

Coded UI Test (CUIT) is a relatively new automation tool in the software market. It was made available as part of the Visual Studio 2010 update. The product has undergone a lot of enhancements and its new version has been released as part of Visual Studio 2013. Software code can be easily reviewed and debugged in Visual Studio. It also has an IntelliSense code completion feature, which helps in generating code faster. Coded UI supports high level programming languages C# and Visual Basic .NET.

A high level diagram illustrating the layers of Coded UI appears below -

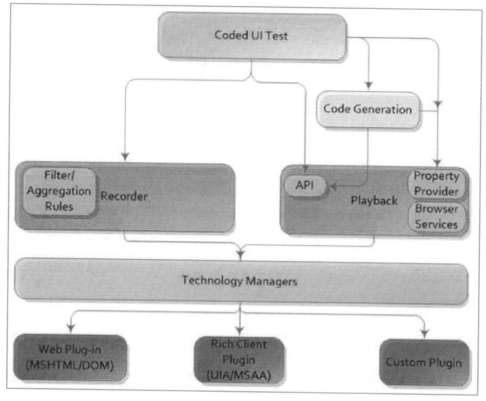

Figure 4.2 – Coded UI Framework

The above diagram has the following components -

- The lowest layer is of technology managers. A technology manager is a module that understands the corresponding UI technology and provides the UI technology specific services to the rest of the modules.

    a. **Web Plug-in/DOM** -The web implementation is utilized to access the DOM in a web browser. It supports Internet Explorer and cross browser playback in Chrome and Firefox, utilizing some additional plugins.

    b. **Rich Client/MSAA/UIA** - MSAA is a COM based technology, which was integrated into Microsoft Windows Operating System starting with Microsoft Windows 98. MSAA is utilized to automate Win Forms applications.UIA was introduced with Microsoft .NET framework.

- Next up is the **Technology Managers** (abstraction) layer which helps abstract rest of the code from various technologies.

- After this are the recorder and playback modules.

    a. **Recorder** -The recorder first records the raw steps and based on the filter\ aggregation rules, these raw steps are converted into filtered steps. These steps are the required workflow designed by the user.

b. Playback - The playback has the public API (.NET) for the users to use. Apart from this, it also has property provider (UI control properties) to give information on properties supported by each control and browser service for browser specific operations like *maximize browser window.*

c. The top layer is the Coded UI Test (or VS client) which generates code out of the recording. To do this, it uses information provided to it by the property provider for each control. If you prefer to hand-code the automation script, you can do so using the API.

We can also use the **Test Runner** feature of Microsoft test Manager which uses the above functionality to do Fast Forwarding for manual tests. This "interprets" the recording on the fly and calls the appropriate API on the playback side.

4.3 Supported Configurations and Platforms for Coded UI Tests

To install and use Coded UI, the computer must have one of the following test platforms installed:

- Microsoft Visual Studio 2015 Enterprise
- Microsoft Visual Studio 2013 Premium/Ultimate/Test Professional edition
- Microsoft Visual Studio 2012 Premium/Ultimate/Test Professional edition
- Microsoft Visual Studio 2010 Premium/Ultimate/Test Professional edition (Service Pack 1)
- Microsoft Test Manager 2010, 2012 or 2013
- Microsoft Test Agent 2010, 2012 or 2013

In this book, we are using Visual Studio 2015 Enterprise. The supported configurations and platforms for coded UI tests for Visual Studio Enterprise are listed in the following table. These configurations also apply to action recordings created by Test Runner (Microsoft Test Manager).

> **Note:** The supporting versions of .NET/Visual Studio can be found at MSDN website. Find more at - https://msdn.microsoft.com/en-us/library/dd380742.aspx.

Supported Configurations

Configuration	Supported
Operating Systems	Windows 7
	Windows Server 2008 R2
	Windows 8
	Windows 10
32-bit / 64-bit Support	32-bit Windows that is running 32-bit Microsoft Test Manager can test 32-bit applications.
	64-bit Windows that is running 32-bit Microsoft Test Manager can test 32-bit WOW Applications that have UI Synchronization.
	64-bit Windows that is running 32-bit Microsoft Test Manager can test 64-bit Windows Forms and WPF Applications that do not have UI Synchronization.
Architecture	x86 and x64
	Note: Internet Explorer is not supported in 64-bit mode except when running under Windows 8 or later versions.
.NET	.NET 2.0, 3.0, 3.5, 4 and 4.5.
	Note: Microsoft Test Manager and Visual Studio will both require .NET 4 to operate. However, applications developed by using the listed .NET versions are supported.

Platform Support

Platform	Level of Support
Windows Phone Apps	Only WinRT-XAML based Phone apps are supported.
Windows Store Apps	Only XAML-based Store apps are supported.
Universal Windows Apps	Only XAML-based Universal Windows Apps on Phone and Desktop are supported.

Edge	Not supported
Internet Explorer 8	Fully supported.
Internet Explorer 9	Fully Supported.
Internet Explorer 10	Support for HTML5 in Internet Explorer 9 and Internet Explorer 10: Coded UI tests support record, playback, and validation of the HTML5 controls: Audio, Video, Progress Bar and Slider. For more information, see Using HTML5 Controls in Coded UI Tests.
Note: Internet Explorer 10 is only supported on the desktop.	Warning: If you create a coded UI test in Internet Explorer 10, it might not run using Internet Explorer 9 or Internet Explorer 8. This is because Internet Explorer 10 includes HTML5 controls such as Audio, Video, Progress Bar, and Slider. These HTML5 controls are not recognized by Internet Explorer 9 or Internet Explorer 8. Likewise, your coded UI test using Internet Explorer 9 might include some HTML5 controls that also will not be recognized by Internet Explorer 8.
Internet Explorer 11	**Support for Internet Explorer 10 Spell Checking:** Internet Explorer 10 includes spell checking capabilities for all text boxes. This allows you to choose from a list of suggested corrections. Coded UI Test will ignore user actions like selecting an alternative spelling suggestion. Only the final text typed into the text box will be recorded.
	The following actions are recorded for coded UI test that use the spell checking control: Add to Dictionary, Copy, Select All, Add To Dictionary, and Ignore.
Internet Explorer 11 is only supported on the desktop.	**Support for 64-bit Internet Explorer running under Windows 8:** Previously, 64-bit versions of Internet Explorer were not supported for recording and playback. With Windows 8 and Visual Studio 2012, coded UI tests have been enabled for 64-bit versions of Internet Explorer.
	Warning: 64-bit support for Internet Explorer applies only when you are running Windows 8 or later.

	Support for Pinned Sites in Internet Explorer 9: In Internet Explorer 9, pinned sites were introduced. With Pinned Sites, you can get to your favorite sites directly from the Windows taskbar—without having to open Internet Explorer first. Coded UI tests can now generate intent-aware actions on pinned sites. For more information about pinned sites, see Pinned Sites.
	Support for Internet Explorer 9 Semantic Tags: Internet Explorer 9 introduced the following semantic tags: section, nav, article, aside, hgroup, header, footer, figure, figcaption and mark. Coded UI tests ignore all of these semantic tags while recording. You can add assertions on these tags using the Coded UI Test Builder. You can use the navigation dial in the Coded UI Test Builder to navigate to any of these elements and view their properties.
	Seamless Handling of White Space Characters between Versions of Internet Explorer: There are differences in the handling of white space characters among Internet Explorer 8, Internet Explorer 9, and Internet Explorer 10. Coded UI Test handles these differences seamlessly. Therefore, a coded UI test created in Internet Explorer 8 for example, will play back successfully in Internet Explorer 9 and Internet Explorer 10.
	The Notification Area of Internet Explorer Are Now Recorded With the "Continue on Error" Attribute Set: All actions on the Notification Area of Internet Explorer are now recorded with the "Continue on Error" attribute set. If the notification bar does not appear during playback, the actions on it will be ignored and coded UI test will continue with the next action.
Windows Forms and WPF third party controls	Fully supported.
	To enable third party controls in Windows Forms and WPF applications, you must add references and code.
Internet Explorer 6	Not supported.
Internet Explorer 7	

Chrome	Recording of action steps is not supported. Coded UI Tests can be played back on Chrome and Firefox browsers with Visual Studio 2012 Update 4 or later.
Firefox	
Opera	Not supported.
Safari	
Silverlight	Not supported.
	For Visual Studo 2013 however, you can download the Microsoft Visual Studio 2013 Coded UI Test Plugin for Silverlight from the Visual Studio Gallery.
Flash/Java	Not supported.
Windows Forms 2.0 and later	Fully supported.
	Note: NetFx controls are fully supported, but not all third-party controls are supported.
WPF 3.5 and later	Fully supported.
	Note: NetFx controls are fully supported, but not all third-party controls are supported.
Windows Win32	May work with some known issues, but not officially supported.
MFC	Partially supported.
SharePoint	Fully supported.
Office Client Applications	Not supported.
Dynamics CRM web client	Fully supported.
Dynamics (Ax) 2012 client	Action recording and playback are partially supported.
SAP	Not supported.

Citrix/Terminal Services	Microsoft doesn't recommend recording actions on a terminal server. The recorder doesn't support running multiple instances at the same time.
PowerBuilder	Partially supported.
	The support is to the extent accessibility is enabled for PowerBuilder controls.

4.4 Installation Requirements for Coded UI

As discussed above, Coded UI is available post Visual Studio 2010. For the purpose of this book, we will be using Visual Studio 2015 Enterprise (the latest version). Visual Studio is a licensed software from Microsoft. We will therefore be using the trial version of the software.

Before installing Visual Studio, let us have a look at the operating and hardware requirements.

Supported Operating Systems

- Windows 10
- Windows 8.1
- Windows 8
- Windows 7 Service Pack 1
- Windows Server 2012 R2
- Windows Server 2012
- Windows Server 2008 R2 SP1

Hardware Requirements

- 1.6 GHz or faster processor
- 1 GB of RAM (1.5 GB if running on a virtual machine)
- 10 GB of available hard disk space
- 5400 RPM hard disk drive
- DirectX 9-capable video card that runs at 1024 x 768 or higher display resolution

> **Note:** We will be using Web Installer to download Visual Studio. An internet connection will be required to install the software.

To download and install Visual Studio Enterprise, follow these steps –

1. Visit the webpage https://www.visualstudio.com/en-us/downloads/download-visual-studio-vs.aspx.

2. Click on **Download Enterprise Trial** as shown below.

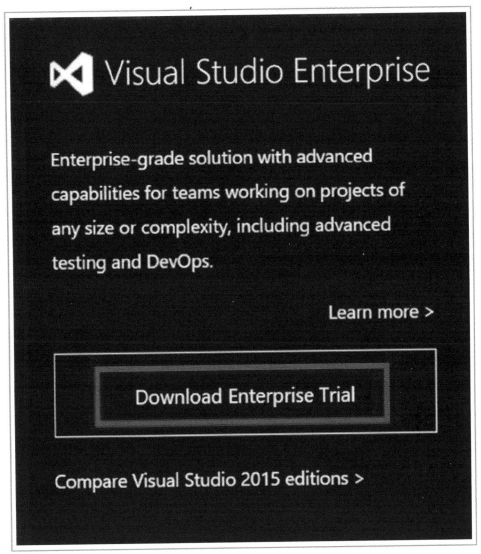

Figure 4.3 –Visual Studio Installation Page

3. Once you click on this link, the installer file *vs_enterprise_ENU.exe* will be downloaded on your system.

4. Double-click this file to complete your installation.

5. The installer will start as shown below.

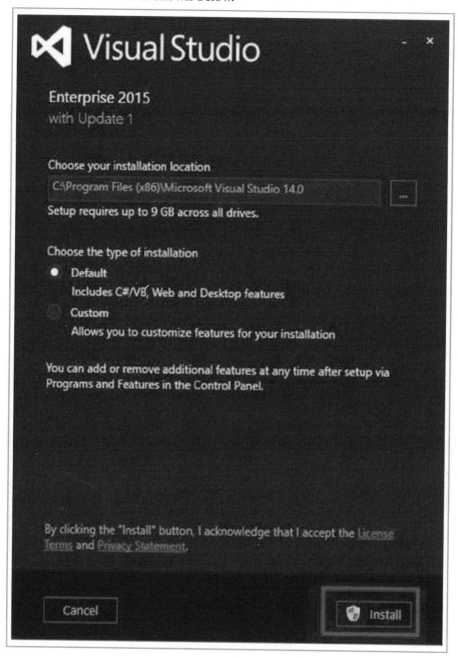

Figure 4.4 – Visual Studio Installation started

6. Click on the **Install** button.

7. Once you click on the Install button and click Yes for administrative privileges, the installer will start downloading Visual Studio.

8. The installer will acquire the necessary installation files from internet.

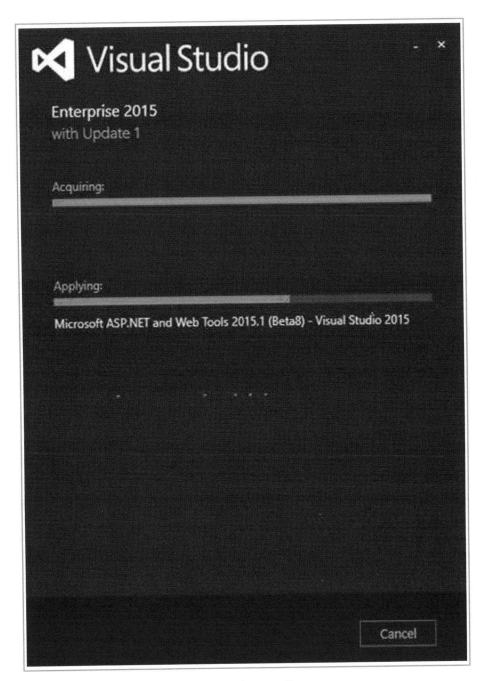

Figure 4.5 – Visual Studio Installation in progress

9. Once, the setup is complete you will be shown the same by the installer. The installation process takes around 30-45 minutes.

10. System restart is required for successful installation of Visual Studio.

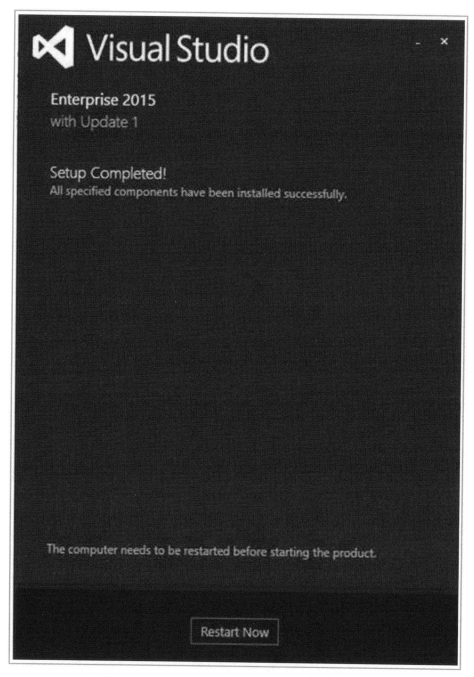

Figure 4.6 – Visual Studio Installation Complete

11. Once the system is restarted, search for **Visual Studio** on your system and click on the executable file as shown below.

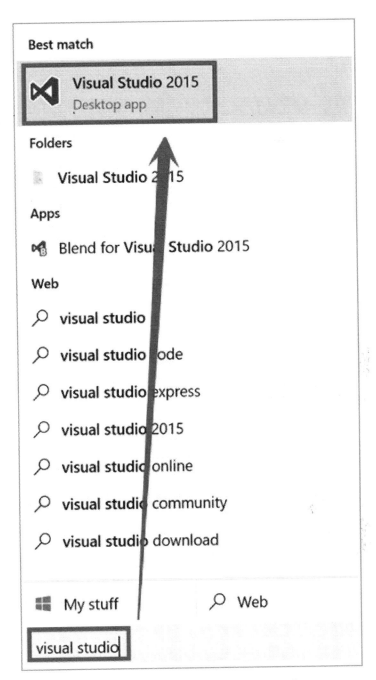

Figure 4.7 – Visual Studio Icon after Installation

12. When Visual Studio is started for the first time, it asks you to sign in using your Windows Azure account. If you do not have an account, you can choose to skip this step.

Figure 4.8 – Visual Studio first time launch

13. Visual Studio will then ask you to choose a color theme for your IDE. You can select any one of these and click on the **Start Visual Studio** button.

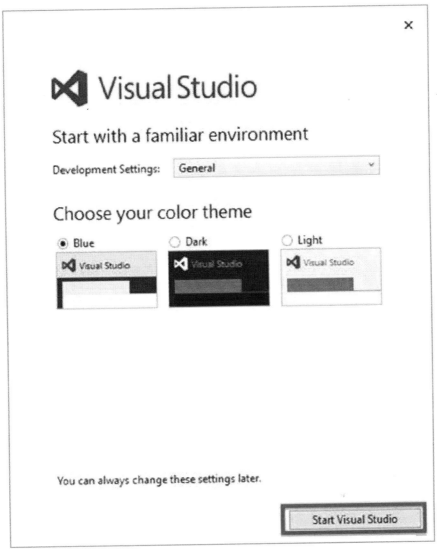

Figure 4.9 – Visual Studio color theme selection

14. Visual Studio would then prepare itself for first time use. You would see this image.

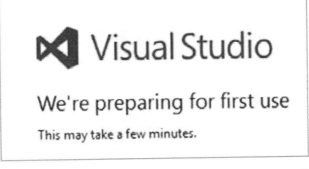

Figure 4.10 – Visual Studio preparing before first launch

15. Once started, the environment of Visual Studio would look like this –

Figure 4.11 – Visual Studio homepage

Note: By default, Visual Studio comes with 30 days' trial period. However, if you register with Microsoft on the Visual Studio IDE, the trial is extended to 90 days.

In Chapter 6, we will be using Visual Studio IDE to create our first Coded UI script. Before that, we will go through some basic C# and object oriented programming concepts.

ᴇ⁄ᴐ

5.

C# Basics

Since we will be focusing on C# as a programming language in Coded UI, we need to be comfortable with the basics of C#. As part of this chapter, we will discuss the basic concepts in .NET and C# language, syntax for basic C# statements, exception handling and the concept of classes and objects.

We do not expect you to be a perfect programmer and C# expert to work with Coded UI as we will be using core .NET concepts and basic C#. So be confident and let us understand these concepts!

Key objectives

- Object-oriented Programming Concepts
- Language and Syntax Basics
- Object, Classes and methods
- Exception Handling

5.1 Object-oriented Programming Concepts

If you've never used an object-oriented programming language before, you'll need to learn a few basic concepts before you can begin writing any code. This chapter will introduce you to terms like objects, classes, inheritance, interfaces, and packages. Each topic focuses on how these concepts relate to the real world, while simultaneously providing an introduction to the syntax of the C# programming language.

> **Note:** Since this book focuses on Coded UI using C#, we willbe working on C# syntax only.

What Is an Object?

Objects are a key to understanding *'object-oriented'* technology. Look around right now and you'll find many examples of real-world objects: Your dog, your desk, your television set, your bicycle.

Real-world objects share two characteristics: They all have *'state'* and *'behavior'*. Dogs have state (name, color, breed, hungry) and behavior (barking, fetching, wagging tail). Bicycles also have state (current gear, current pedal cadence, current speed) and behavior (changing gear, changing pedal cadence, applying brakes). Identifying the state and behavior for real-world objects is a great way to begin thinking in terms of object-oriented programming.

Take a minute right now to observe the real-world objects that are in your immediate area. For each object that you see, ask yourself two questions: "What possible states can this object be in?" and "What possible behavior can this object perform?" Make sure to write down your observations. As you do, you'll notice that real-world objects vary in complexity; your desktop lamp may have only two possible states (on and off) and two possible behaviors (turn on, turn off), but your desktop radio might have additional states (on, off, current volume, current station) and behavior (turn on, turn off, increase volume, decrease volume, seek, scan, and tune). You may also notice that some objects, in turn, will also contain other objects. These real-world observations all translate into the world of object-oriented programming.

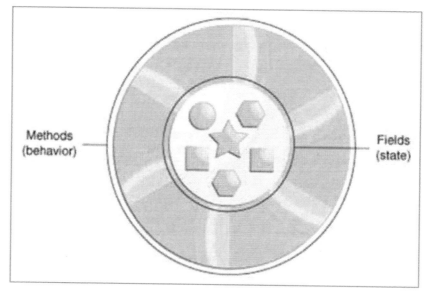

Figure 5-1 - A software object

Software objects are conceptually similar to real-world objects: they too consist of state and related behavior. An object stores its state in 'fields' (variables in some programming languages) and exposes its behavior through 'methods' (functions in some programming languages). Methods operate on an object's internal state and serve as the primary mechanism for object-to-object communication. Hiding internal state and requiring all interaction to be performed through an object's methods is known as '***data encapsulation***'— a fundamental principle of object-oriented programming.

Consider a bicycle, for example:

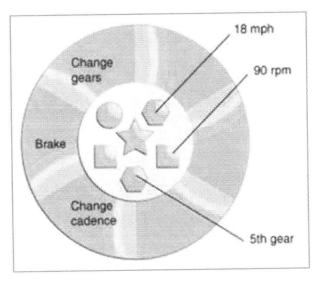

Figure 5-2 - A bicycle modelled as a software object

By attributing state (current speed, current pedal cadence, and current gear) and providing methods for changing that state, the object remains in control of how the outside world is allowed to use it. For example, if the bicycle only has 6 gears, a method to change gears could reject any value that is less than 1 or greater than 6.

Bundling code into individual software objects provide a number of benefits, including:

1. **Modularity**: The Source code for an object can be written and maintained independently of the Source code for other objects. Once created, an object can be easily passed around inside the system.

2. **Information-hiding**: By interacting only with an object's methods, the details of its internal implementation remain hidden from the outside world.

3. **Code re-use**: If an object already exists (perhaps written by another software developer), you can use that object in your program. This allows specialists to implement/test/debug complex, task-specific objects, which you can then trust to run in your own code.

4. **Plug-ability and debugging ease**: If a particular object turns out to be problematic, you can simply remove it from your application and plug in a different object as its replacement. This is analogous to fixing mechanical problems in the real world. If a bolt breaks, you replace it, not the entire machine.

What Is a Class?

A class is a blueprint or prototype from which objects are created. This section defines a class that models the state and behavior of a real-world object. It intentionally focuses on the basics and shows how a simple class can model state and behavior.

In the real world, you'll often find many objects of the same kind. There may be thousands of bicycles in existence, all of the same make and model. Each bicycle was built from the same set of blueprints and therefore contains the same components. In object-oriented terms, we say that your bicycle is an *instance* of the *class of objects* known as bicycles. A *class* is the blueprint from which individual objects are created.

The following 'Bicycle' class is one possible implementation of a bicycle:

```
class Bicycle {

    int cadence = 0;
    int speed = 0;
    int gear = 1;

    public void ChangeCadence(int newValue) {
        cadence = newValue;
    }

    public void ChangeGear(int newValue) {
        gear = newValue;
    }

    public void SpeedUp(int increment) {
        speed = speed + increment;
    }

    public void ApplyBrakes(int decrement) {
        speed = speed - decrement;
    }

    public void PrintStates() {
    Console.WriteLine("cadence:" +
            cadence + " speed:" +
            speed + " gear:" + gear);
    }
}
```

The syntax of the C# programming language will look new to you, but the design of this class is based on the previous discussion of bicycle objects. The field's cadence,speed, and gear represent the object's state, and the methods (changeCadence, changeGear, speedup,. etc.) define its interaction with the outside world.

You may have noticed that the 'Bicycle' class does not contain a 'main' method. That's because it's not a complete application; it's just the blueprint for bicycles that might be '*used*' in an application. The responsibility of creating and using new 'Bicycle' objects belong to some other class in your application.

Here's a BicycleDemo class that creates two separate 'Bicycle' objects and invokes their methods:

```csharp
class BicycleDemo {

  public static void Main(string[] args) {


    // Create two different

    // Bicycle objects

    Bicycle bike1 = new Bicycle();

    Bicycle bike2 = new Bicycle();

    // Invoke methods on

    // those objects

    bike1.ChangeCadence(50);

    bike1.SpeedUp(10);

    bike1.ChangeGear(2);

    bike1.PrintStates();


    bike2.ChangeCadence(50);

    bike2.SpeedUp(10);

    bike2.ChangeGear(2);

    bike2.ChangeCadence(40);

    bike2.SpeedUp(10);

bike2.ChangeGear(3);

    bike2.PrintStates();

  }

}
```

The output of this test prints the ending pedal cadence, speed, and gear for the two bicycles:

cadence:50 speed:10 gear:2

cadence:40 speed:20 gear:3

What Is Inheritance?

Inheritance provides a powerful and natural mechanism for organizing and structuring your software. This section explains how classes inherit state and behavior from their base classes, and explains how to derive one class from another using the simple syntax provided by C# programming language.

Different kinds of objects often have a certain amount in common with each other. Mountain bikes, road bikes, and tandem bikes, for example, all share the characteristics of bicycles (current speed, current pedal cadence, current gear). Yet each also contain additional features that make them different: tandem bicycles have two seats and two sets of handlebars; road bikes have drop handlebars; some mountain bikes have an additional chain ring, giving them a lower gear ratio.

Object-oriented programming allows classes to *inherit* commonly used state and behavior from other classes. In this example, 'Bicycle' now becomes the *base class* of MountainBike, RoadBike, and TandemBike. In the C# programming language, each class is allowed to have one direct base class, and each base class has the potential for an unlimited number of *derived classes*:

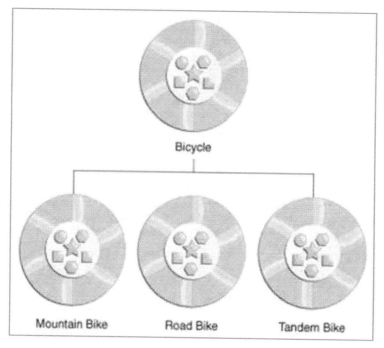

Figure 5-3 - A hierarchy of bicycle classes

The syntax for creating a derived class is simple. At the beginning of your class declaration, use the ':' symbol, followed by the name of the class to inherit from:

```
class MountainBike : Bicycle {


    // new fields and methods defining

    // a mountain bike would go here



}
```

This gives 'MountainBike' the same fields and methods as 'Bicycle', yet allows its code to focus exclusively on the features that make it unique. This makes code for your derived classes easy to read. However, you must take care to properly document the state and behavior that each base class defines, since that code will not appear in the source file of each derived class.

What Is an Interface?

An interface is a contract between a class and the outside world. When a class implements an interface, it promises to provide the behavior published by that interface. This section defines a simple interface and explains the necessary changes for any class that implements it.

As you've already learned, objects define their interaction with the outside world through the methods that they expose. Methods form the object's *interface* with the outside world; the buttons on the front of your television set, for example, are the interface between you and the electrical wiring on the other side of its plastic casing. You press the "power" button to turn the television on and off.

In its most common form, an interface is a group of related methods with empty bodies. A bicycle's behavior, if specified as an interface, might appear as follows:

```
interface Bicycle {

    // wheel revolutions per minute
    void ChangeCadence(int newValue);

    void ChangeGear(int newValue);

    void SpeedUp(int increment);

    void ApplyBrakes(int decrement);
}
```

To implement this interface, the name of your class would change (to a particular brand of bicycle, for example, such as ACMEBicycle), and you would use the ':' symbol in the class declaration:

```
class ACMEBicycle : Bicycle {


    // remainder of this class

    // implemented as before

}
```

Implementing an interface allows a class to become more formal about the behavior it promises to provide. Interfaces form a contract between the class and the outside world, and this contract is enforced at build time by the compiler. If your class claims to implement an interface, all methods defined by that interface must appear in its source code before the class will successfully compile.

What Is a Namespace?

A namespace is designed for providing a way to keep one set of names separate from another. The class names declared in one namespace do not conflict with the same class names declared in another.

Conceptually you can think of namespaces as being similar to different folders on your computer. You might keep HTML pages in one folder, images in another, and scripts or applications in yet another. Because software written in the C# programming language can be composed of hundreds or *thousands* of individual classes, it makes sense to keep things organized by placing related classes and interfaces into namespaces.

What Is .NET Class library?

The .NET Framework class library is a library of classes, interfaces, and value types that are included in the Microsoft .NET Framework SDK. This library provides access to system functionality and is designed to be the foundation on which .NET Framework applications, components, and controls are built.

For example, a 'String' object contains state and behavior for character strings; a 'File' object allows a programmer to easily create, delete, inspect, compare, or modify a file on the file system; a 'Socket' object allows for the creation and use of network sockets; various GUI objects control buttons and checkboxes and anything else related to graphical user interfaces.

There are literally thousands of classes to choose from. This allows you, the programmer, to focus on the design of your particular application, rather than the infrastructure required to make it work.

The MSDN (Microsoft Developer Network) contains the complete listing for all namespaces, interfaces, classes, fields, and methods supplied by the .NET platform (https://msdn.microsoft.com/en-us/library/mt472912(v=vs.110).aspx). Load the page in your browser and bookmark it. As a programmer, it will become your single most important piece of reference documentation.

5.2 Language and Syntax Basics

Variables

You've already learned that objects store their state in fields. However, the C# programming language also uses the term "variable". Let's discuss this relationship, plus variable naming rules and conventions, basic data types (primitive types, character strings, and arrays), default values, and literals.

```
int cadence = 0;

int speed = 0;

int gear = 1;
```

Primitive Data Types

The C# programming language is statically-typed, which means that all variables must first be declared before they can be used. This involves stating the variable's type and name, as you've already seen:

```
int gear = 1;
```

The following chart summarizes the primitive data types and their default values.

Data Type	Default Value (for fields)
Byte	0
Short	0
Int	0
Long	0
Float	0.0f
Double	0.0d
Char	'\x0000'

String (or any object)	Null
Boolean	False

The C# programming language defines the following kinds of variables:

- Instance Variables (Non-Static Fields): Technically speaking, objects store their individual states in "non-static fields", that is, fields declared without the **static** keyword. Non-static fields are also known as ***instance variables*** because their values are unique to each *instance* of a class (to each object, in other words); the current Speed of one bicycle is independent from the current Speed of another.

- Class Variables (Static Fields): A *class variable* is any field declared with the static modifier; this tells the compiler that there is exactly one copy of this variable in existence, regardless of how many times the class has been instantiated. A field defining the number of gears for a particular kind of bicycle could be marked as static since conceptually the same number of gears will apply to all instances. The code 'static int numGears = 6'; would create such a static field. Additionally, the keyword 'final' could be added to indicate that the number of gears will never change.

- Local Variables: Similar to how an object stores its state in fields, a method will often store its temporary state in '*local variables*'. The syntax for declaring a local variable is similar to declaring a field (for example, 'int count = 0';). There is no special keyword designating a variable as local; that determination comes entirely from the location in which the variable is declared — which is between the opening and closing braces of a method. As such, local variables are only visible to the methods in which they are declared; they are not accessible from the rest of the class.

- Parameters: You've already seen examples of parameters in the Bicycle class. Recall that the signature for the main method is public static void Main(string[] args). Here, the args variable is the parameter to this method. The important thing to remember is that parameters are always classified as "variables" not "fields". This applies to other parameter-accepting constructs as well (such as constructors and exception handlers) that you'll learn about later in this book.

Naming Conventions

Every programming language has its own set of rules and conventions for the kinds of names that you're allowed to use, and the C# programming language is no different. The rules and conventions for naming your variables can be summarized as follows:

- **Do** use meaningful names for various types, functions, variables, constructs and data structures. Their use should be plainly discernable from their name alone.

- Single-character variables should only be used as counters (i, j) or as coordinates (x, y, z). As a rule-of-thumb a variable should have a more descriptive name as its scope increases.

- **You should not** use shortenings or contractions as parts of identifier names. For example, use "GetWindow" rather than "GetWin". For functions of common types, thread procs, window procedures, dialog procedures use the common suffixes for these "ThreadProc", "DialogProc", "WndProc".

Arrays

An *array* is a container object that holds a fixed number of values of a single type. The length of an array is established when the array is created. After creation, its length is fixed. This section discusses arrays in greater detail.

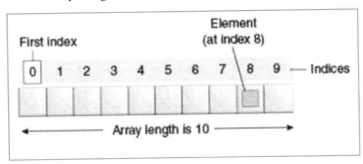

Figure 5-4 -   An array of ten elements

Each item in an array is called an *element*, and each element is accessed by its numerical *index*. As shown in the above illustration, numbering begins with 0. The 9th element, for example, would therefore be accessed at index 8. The following program, ArrayDemo, creates an array of integers, puts some values in it, and prints each value to standard output.

```
class ArrayDemo {

  public static void Main(string[] args) {

// declares an array of integers

    int[] anArray;


// allocates memory for 10 integers

    anArray = new int[10];


// initialize first element

    anArray[0] = 100;

// initialize second element

    anArray[1] = 200;

// etc.

    anArray[2] = 300;
```

```
        anArray[3] = 400;

        anArray[4] = 500;

        anArray[5] = 600;

        anArray[6] = 700;

        anArray[7] = 800;

        anArray[8] = 900;

        anArray[9] = 1000;

    Console.WriteLine("Element at index 0: "
                    + anArray[0]);
    Console.WriteLine("Element at index 1: "
                    + anArray[1]);
    Console.WriteLine("Element at index 2: "
                    + anArray[2]);
    Console.WriteLine("Element at index 3: "
                    + anArray[3]);
    Console.WriteLine("Element at index 4: "
                    + anArray[4]);
    Console.WriteLine("Element at index 5: "
                    + anArray[5]);
    Console.WriteLine("Element at index 6: "
                    + anArray[6]);
    Console.WriteLine("Element at index 7: "
                    + anArray[7]);
    Console.WriteLine("Element at index 8: "
                    + anArray[8]);
    Console.WriteLine("Element at index 9: "
                    + anArray[9]);
    }
}
```

The output from this program is:

Element at index 0: 100

Element at index 1: 200

Element at index 2: 300

Element at index 3: 400

Element at index 4: 500

Element at index 5: 600

Element at index 6: 700

Element at index 7: 800

Element at index 8: 900

Element at index 9: 1000

In a real-world programming situation, you would probably use one of the supported *looping constructs* to iterate through each element of the array, rather than write each line individually as shown above. However, this example clearly illustrates the array syntax.

Declaring a Variable to Refer to an Array

The above program declares "anArray" with the following line of code:

```
// declares an array of integers
int[] anArray;
```

Like declarations for variables of other types, an array declaration has two components: the array's type and the array's name. An array's type is written as type[], where type is the data type of the contained elements; the square brackets are special symbols indicating that this variable holds an array. The size of the array is not part of its type (which is why the brackets are empty). An array's name can be anything you want, provided that it follows the rules and conventions as previously discussed in the naming section. As with variables of other types, the declaration does not actually create an array — it simply tells the compiler that this variable will hold an array of the specified type.

Similarly, you can declare arrays of other types:

```
byte[] anArrayOfBytes;
short[] anArrayOfShorts;
long[] anArrayOfLongs;
float[] anArrayOfFloats;
double[] anArrayOfDoubles;
```

```
char[] anArrayOfChars;
```

```
String[] anArrayOfStrings;
```

Creating, Initializing, and Accessing an Array

One way to create an array is with the new operator. The next statement in the ArrayDemo program allocates an array with enough memory for ten integer elements and assigns the array to the anArray variable.

```
// create an array of integers
```

```
anArray = new int[10];
```

The next few lines assign values to each element of the array:

```
anArray[0] = 100; // initialize first element
```

```
anArray[1] = 200; // initialize second element
```

```
anArray[2] = 300; // etc.
```

Each array element is accessed by its numerical index:

```
Console.WriteLine("Element 1 at index 0: " + anArray[0]);
```

```
Console.WriteLine("Element 2 at index 1: " + anArray[1]);
```

```
Console.WriteLine("Element 3 at index 2: " + anArray[2]);
```

Alternatively, you can use the shortcut syntax to create and initialize an array:

```
int[] anArray = {
    100, 200, 300,
    400, 500, 600,
    700, 800, 900, 1000
};
```

Here the length of the array is determined by the number of values provided between{and}.

You can also declare an array of arrays (also known as a multidimension alarray) by using two or more sets of square brackets, such asString[][] names. Each element, therefore, must be accessed by a corresponding number of index values.

In the C# programming language, a multidimensional array is simply an array whose components are themselves arrays. This is unlike arrays in C or Fortran. A consequence of this is that the rows are allowed to vary in length, as shown in the followingMultiDimArr ayDemoprogram:

```
class MultiDimArrayDemo {

    public static void Main(string[] args) {

        String[][] names = {

            {"Mr. ", "Mrs. ", "Ms. "},

            {"Smith", "Jones"}

        };
        // Mr. Smith
Console.WriteLine(names[0][0] + names[1][0]);

        // Ms. Jones
Console.WriteLine(names[0][2] + names[1][1]);

    }

}
```

The output from this program is:

Mr. Smith

Ms. Jones

Finally, you can use the built-in length property to determine the size of any array. The code

Console.WriteLine(anArray.Length); -will print the array's size to standard output.

Operators

Now that you've learned how to declare and initialize variables, you probably want to know how to use them. Learning the operators of the C# programming language is a good place to start. Operators are special symbols that perform specific operations on one, two, or three *operands*, and then return a result. The following is a quick reference for operators supported by the C# programming language.

Assignment Operators

=	Simple assignment operator, Assigns values from right side operands to left side operand
+=	Add AND assignment operator, It adds right operand to the left operand and assign the result to left operand

-=	Subtract AND assignment operator, It subtracts right operand from the left operand and assign the result to left operand
*=	Multiply AND assignment operator, It multiplies right operand with the left operand and assign the result to left operand
/=	Divide AND assignment operator, It divides left operand with the right operand and assign the result to left operand
%=	Modulus AND assignment operator, It takes modulus using two operands and assign the result to left operand
<<=	Left shift AND assignment operator
>>=	Right shift AND assignment operator
&=	Bitwise AND assignment operator
^=	bitwise exclusive OR and assignment operator
|=	bitwise inclusive OR and assignment operator

Arithmetic Operators

+ Additive operator (also used for String concatenation)

- Subtraction operator

* Multiplication operator

/ Division operator

% Remainder operator

Unary Operators

+ Unary plus operator; indicates positive value (numbers are positive without this)

- Unary minus operator; negates an expression

++ Increment operator; increment a value by 1

-- Decrement operator; decrements a value by 1

! Logical complement operator; inverts the value of a boolean

Equality and Relational Operators

== Equal to

!=   Not equal to

>   Greater than

>=   Greater than or equal to

<   Less than

<=   Less than or equal to

Conditional Operators

&&   Conditional-AND

|| Conditional-OR

?   Ternary (shorthand for if-then-else statement)

Control Flow Statements

The statements inside your source files are generally executed from top to bottom, in the order that they appear. *Control flow statements*, however, break up the flow of execution by employing decision making, looping, and branching, enabling your program to *conditionally* execute particular blocks of code. This section describes the decision-making statements (if, if-else, switch), the looping statements (for, while, do-while), and the branching statements (break, continue, return) supported by the C# programming language.

The If-elseif-else Statement

if(condition A)   {// do this   }

elseif(condition B)   { //do this   }

else   { //do this   }

The control will go to one of the block of statements depending upon the given condition.

```
class IfElseDemo {

  public static void Main(string[] args) {


    int testscore = 76;

    char grade;


    if (testscore >= 90) {

      grade = 'A';
```

```
    } else if (testscore >= 80) {

        grade = 'B';

    } else if (testscore >= 70) {

        grade = 'C';

    } else if (testscore >= 60) {

        grade = 'D';

    } else {

        grade = 'F';

    }

Console.WriteLine("Grade = " + grade);

    }

}
```

The output from the program is:

```
Grade = C
```

The Switch Statement

Unlike if-then and if-then-else statements, the switch statement can have a number of possible execution paths. A switch works with the byte, short, char, and int primitive data types. It also works with enumerated types(discussed in Enum Types), the String class, and a few special classes that wrap certain primitive types: Character, Byte, Short, and Integer (discussed in Numbers and Strings).

The following code example, SwitchDemo, declares an int named month whose value represents a month. The code displays the name of the month, based on the value of month, using the switch statement.

```
public class SwitchDemo {

    public static void Main(string[] args) {


        int month = 8;

    string monthString;

        switch (month) {

            case 1:  monthString = "January";

                    break;
```

```csharp
        case 2:  monthString = "February";
            break;
        case 3:  monthString = "March";
            break;
        case 4:  monthString = "April";
            break;
        case 5:  monthString = "May";
            break;
        case 6:  monthString = "June";
            break;
        case 7:  monthString = "July";
            break;
        case 8:  monthString = "August";
            break;
        case 9:  monthString = "September";
            break;
        case 10: monthString = "October";
            break;
        case 11: monthString = "November";
            break;
        case 12: monthString = "December";
            break;
        default: monthString = "Invalid month";
            break;
    }
    Console.WriteLine(monthString);
    }
}
```

In this case, August is printed to standard output.

Looping Statements

The while and do-while Statements

The while statement executes a block of statements while a particular condition is true. Its syntax can be expressed as:

```
while (expression) {

    statement(s)

}
```

The while statement evaluates an expression, which must return a Boolean value. If the expression evaluates to true, the while statement executes the statement(s) in the while block. The while statement continues testing the expression and executing its block until the expression evaluates to false. Using the while statement to print the values from 1 through 10 can be accomplished as in the following **WhileDemo** program:

```
class WhileDemo {

    public static void Main(string[] args){

        int count = 1;

        while (count < 11) {
Console.WriteLine("Count is: " + count);

            count++;

        }

    }

}
```

You can implement an infinite loop using the while statement as follows:

```
while (true){

    // your code goes here

}
```

The C# programming language also provides a do-while statement, which can be expressed as follows:

```
do {

    statement(s)

} while (expression);
```

The difference between do-while and while is that do-while evaluates its expression at the bottom of the loop instead of the top. Therefore, the statements within the do block are always executed at least once, as shown in the following DoWhileDemo program:

```
class DoWhileDemo {
    public static void Main(string[] args){
        int count = 1;
        do {
Console.WriteLine("Count is: " + count);
            count++;
        } while (count < 11);
    }
}
```

The for Statement

The **for statement** provides a compact way to iterate over a range of values. Programmers often refer to it as the "for loop" because of the way in which it repeatedly loops until a particular condition is satisfied. The syntax of the **for statement** can be expressed as follows:

```
for (initialization; termination;
increment) {
statement(s)
}
```

When using this version of the for statement, keep in mind that:

- The initialization expression initializes the loop; it's executed once, as the loop begins
- When the termination expression evaluates to false, the loop terminates
- The increment expression is invoked after each iteration through the loop; it is perfectly acceptable for this expression to increment or decrement a value

The following program,**ForDemo**, uses the general form of the for statement to print the numbers 1 through 10 to standard output:

```
class ForDemo {

    public static void Main(string[] args){

        for(int i=1; i<11; i++){

Console.WriteLine("Count is: " + i.ToString());

        }

    }

}
```

The output of this program is:

Count is: 1

Count is: 2

Count is: 3

Count is: 4

Count is: 5

Count is: 6

Count is: 7

Count is: 8

Count is: 9

Count is: 10

Miscellaneous Statements

The return Statement

The last of the branching statements is the return statement. The return statement exits from the current method, and control flow returns to where the method was invoked. The return statement has two forms: one that returns a value, and one that doesn't. To return a value, simply put the value (or an expression that calculates the value) after the return keyword.

return ++count;

The data type of the returned value must match the type of the method's declared return value. When a method is declared void, return doesn't return a value or doesn't have a return statement at all.

Comments in C#

C# supports single-line and multi-line comments very similar to C and C++. All characters available inside any comment are ignored by the .NET compiler. You can use double forward slashes - *//* or forward slash and star combination - */* comments */* for comments

```
public class MyCommentsProgram{


/* This is my comments program.

This will print 'Hello World' as the output

This is an example of multi-line comments.

   */



public static void Main(string[]args){

// This is an example of single line comment

/* This is also an example of single line comment. */

Console.WriteLine("Hello World");

}
```

Basic Syntax:

About C# programs, it is very important to keep in mind the following points.

- **Case Sensitivity** –C# is case sensitive, which means identifier **Hello** and **hello** would have different meanings in C#
- **Class Names** -All class names should begin in upper case

  If several words are used to form a name of the class, each inner word's first letter should be in upper case.

  Example*class MyFirstClass*

  Method Names -All method names should begin in upper case

  If several words are used to form the name of the method, then each inner word's first letter should be in upper case.

  Example *public void MethodName()*

- **public static void Main(string args[])** –C# executable programs begin processing from the Main() method which is a mandatory part of every executable C# program

C# Keywords:

The following list shows the reserved words in C#. These reserved words may not be used as a constant or variable or any other identifier name.

abstract	As	base	bool	break	byte	case
catch	Char	checked	class	const	continue	decimal
default	Delegate	do	double	else	enum	event
explicit	Extern	FALSE	finally	fixed	float	for
foreach	Goto	if	implicit	in	in (generic modifier)	int
interface	Internal	is	lock	long	namespace	new
null	Object	operator	out	out (generic modifier)	override	params
private	Protected	public	readonly	ref	return	sbyte
sealed	Short	sizeof	stackalloc	static	string	struct
switch	This	throw	TRUE	try	typeof	uint
ulong	Unchecked	unsafe	ushort	using	virtual	void
volatile	While					

5.3 Working with Classes, Objects and Methods

More on Classes and Objects

With the knowledge you now have of the basics of the C# programming language, you can learn to write your own classes. In this lesson, you will find information about defining your own classes, including declaring member variables, methods, and constructors.

You will learn to use your classes to create objects, and how to use the objects you create.

This lesson also covers nesting classes within other classes, and enumerations.

Declaring Classes

You've seen classes defined in the following way:

```
class MyClass {

    // field, constructor, and

    // method declarations

}
```

This is a *class declaration*. The class body (the area between the braces) contains all the code that provides for the lifecycle of the objects created from the class: Constructors for initializing new objects, declarations for the fields that provide the state of the class and its objects, and methods to implement the behavior of the class and its objects.

The preceding class declaration is a minimal one. It contains only those components of a class declaration that are required. You can provide more information about the class, such as the name of its base class, whether it implements any interfaces, and so on, at the start of the class declaration. For example,

```
class MyClass : MyBaseClass, YourInterface {

    // field, constructor, and

    // method declarations

}
```

means that MyClass is a subclass of MyBaseClass and that it implements the YourInterface interface.

You can also add modifiers like *public* or *private* at the very beginning—so you can see that the opening line of a class declaration can become quite complicated. The modifiers *public* and *private*, which determine what other classes can access MyClass, are discussed later in this lesson. The lesson on interfaces and inheritance will explain more about class declaration. For the moment you do not need to worry about these extra complications.

In general, class declarations can include these components in the following order:

1. Modifiers such as *public*, *private*, and a number of others that you will encounter later

2. The class name, with the initial letter capitalized by convention

3. The name of the class's parent (base class), if any, preceded by the ':' symbol. A class can only *extend* (subclass) one parent.

4. A comma-separated list of interfaces implemented by the class, if any, preceded by the ':' symbol. A class can *implement* more than one interface.

5. The class body, surrounded by braces, {}

Declaring Member Variables

There are several kinds of variables:

- Member variables in a class—these are called *fields*.
- Variables in a method or block of code—these are called *local variables*.
- Variables in method declarations—these are called *parameters*.

The Bicycleclass uses the following lines of code to define its fields:

public	**int**	**cadence;**
(Access modifier)	(Data type)	(Name)

public int gear;

public int speed;

Access Modifiers

The first (left-most) modifier used lets you control what other classes have access to a member field. For the moment, consider only public and private. Other access modifiers will be discussed later.

- public modifier—the field is accessible from all classes
- private modifier—the field is accessible only within its own class

Defining Methods or Functions

Here is an example of a typical method declaration:

```
public double CalculateAnswer(double wingSpan, int numberOfEngines,
                    double length, double grossTons) {
    //do the calculation here

}
```

The only required elements of a method declaration are the method's return type, name, a pair of parentheses,(), and a body between braces,{}.

In general, method declarations have six components in the following order:

1. Modifiers—such as public,private, and others you will learn about later
2. The return type—the data type of the value returned by the method, or void if the method does not return a value
3. The method name—the rules for field names apply to method names as well, but the convention is a little different

4. The parameter list in parenthesis—a comma-delimited list of input parameters, preceded by their data types, enclosed by parentheses,(). If there are no parameters, you must use empty parentheses.

5. An exception list—to be discussed later

6. The method body, enclosed between braces—the method's code, including the declaration of local variables, goes here

Naming a Method or Function

Although a method name can be any legal identifier, code conventions restrict method names. By convention, method names should be a verb in upper-case or a multi-word name that begins with a verb in uppercase, followed by adjectives, nouns, etc. In multi-word names, the first letter of each of the words should be capitalized. Here are some examples:

```
void Print()
```

```
void ProcessItem()
```

Typically, a method has a unique name within its class. However, a method might have the same name as other methods due to *method overloading*.

Overloading Methods

The C# programming language supports *overloading* methods, and C# can distinguish between methods with different *method signatures*. This means that methods within a class can have the same name if they have different parameter lists (there are some qualifications to this that will be discussed in the lesson titled "Interfaces and Inheritance").

Suppose that you have a class that can use calligraphy to draw various types of data (strings, integers, and so on) and that contains a method for drawing each data type. It is cumbersome to use a new name for each method—for example, DrawString, DrawInteger,DrawFloat, and so on. In the C# programming language, you can use the same name for all the drawing methods but pass a different argument list to each method. Thus, the data drawing class might declare four methods named draw, each of which has a different parameter list.

```
public class DataArtist {

    ...

    public void Draw(String s) {

        ...

    }

    public void Draw(int i) {
```

```
        ...

    }

    public void Draw(double f) {

        ...

    }

    public void Draw(int i, double f) {

        ...

    }

}
```

Overloaded methods are differentiated by the number and the type of the arguments passed into the method. In the code sample, Draw(String s) and Draw(int i) are distinct and unique methods because they require different argument types.

You cannot declare more than one method with the same name and the same number and type of arguments, because the compiler cannot tell them apart.

The compiler does not consider return type when differentiating methods, so you cannot declare two methods with the same signature even if they have a different return type.

Providing Constructors for Your Classes

A class contains constructors that are invoked to create objects from the class blueprint. Constructor declarations look like method declarations—except that they use the name of the class and have no return type. For example, Bicycle has one constructor:

```
public Bicycle(int startCadence, int startSpeed, int startGear) {

    gear = startGear;

    cadence = startCadence;

    speed = startSpeed;

}
```

To create a new Bicycle object called myBike, a constructor is called by the new operator:

Bicycle myBike = new Bicycle(30, 0, 8);

new Bicycle(30, 0, 8) creates space in memory for the object and initializes its fields.

Although Bicycle only has one constructor, it could have others, including a no-argument constructor:

```
public Bicycle() {

    gear = 1;

    cadence = 10;

    speed = 0;

}
```

Bicycle yourBike = new Bicycle();invokes the no-argument constructor to create a new Bicycle object called yourBike.

Both constructors could have been declared in Bicycle because they have different argument lists. As with methods, the .NET platform differentiates constructors on the basis of the number of arguments in the list and their types. You cannot write two constructors that have the same number and type of arguments for the same class, because the platform would not be able to tell them apart. Doing so causes a compile-time error.

You don't have to provide any constructors for your class, but you must be careful when doing this. The compiler automatically provides a no-argument, default constructor for any class without constructors. This default constructor will call the no-argument constructor of the base class. In this situation, the compiler will complain if the base class doesn't have a no-argument constructor so you must verify that it does. If your class has no explicit base class, then it has an implicit base class of Object, which *does* have a no-argument constructor.

You can use a base class constructor yourself. The Mountain Bikeclass at the beginning of this lesson did just that. This will be discussed later, in the lesson on interfaces and inheritance.

You can use access modifiers in a constructor's declaration to control which other classes can call the constructor.

Returning a Value from a Method

A method returns to the code that invoked it when it

- completes all the statements in the method,
- reaches a return statement, or
- throws an exception (covered later),

whichever occurs first.

You declare a method's return type in its method declaration. Within the body of the method, you use the return statement to return the value.

Any method declared void doesn't return a value. It does not need to contain a return statement, but it may do so. In such a case, a return statement can be used to branch out of a control flow block and exit the method and is simply used like this:

return;

If you try to return a value from a method that is declared void, you will get a compiler error.

Any method that is not declared void must contain a return statement with a corresponding return value, like this:

return returnValue;

The data type of the return value must match the method's declared return type; you can't return an integer value from a method declared to return a boolean.

The **getArea**() method below returns an integer:

```
// a method for computing the area of the rectangle

    public int GetArea() {

        return width * height;

    }
```

This method returns the integer that the expression 'width*height' evaluates to.

The GetArea method returns a primitive type. A method can also return a reference type. For example, in a program to manipulate Bicycle objects, we might have a method like this:

```
public Bicycle SeeWhosFastest(Bicycle myBike, Bicycle yourBike,

                    Environment env) {

    Bicycle fastest;

    // code to calculate which bike is

    // faster, given each bike's gear

    // and cadence and given the

    // environment (terrain and wind)

    return fastest;

}
```

Using the 'this' Keyword

Within an instance method or a constructor, 'this' is a reference to the *current object*— the object whose method or constructor is being called. You can refer to any member of the current object from within an instance method or a constructor by using 'this'.

Using 'this' with a Field:

The most common reason for using the 'this' keyword is because a field is shadowed by a method or constructor parameter.

For example, the Point class was written like this

```
public class Point {

   public int x = 0;

   public int y = 0;


   //constructor

   public Point(int a, int b) {

      x = a;

      y = b;

   }

}
```

but it could have been written like this:

```
public class Point {

   public int x = 0;

public int y = 0;


   //constructor

   public Point(int x, int y) {

this.x = x;

      this.y = y;

   }

}
```

Each argument to the constructor shadows one of the object's fields — inside the constructor **x** is a local copy of the constructor's first argument. To refer to the Point field **x**, the constructor must use **this.x**.

Using 'this' with a Constructor:

From within a constructor, you can also use the 'this' keyword to call another constructor in the same class. Doing so is called an *explicit constructor invocation*. Here's another Rectangle class, with a different implementation from the one in the Objects section.

```
public class Rectangle {

    private int x, y;

    private int width, height;


    public Rectangle() {
this(0, 0, 0, 0);
    }
    public Rectangle(int width, int height) {
this(0, 0, width, height);
    }
    public Rectangle(int x, int y, int width, int height) {
        this.x = x;
        this.y = y;
        this.width = width;
        this.height = height;
    }
    ...
}
```

This class contains a set of constructors. Each constructor initializes some or all of the rectangle's member variables. The constructors provide a default value for any member variable whose initial value is not provided by an argument. For example, the no-argument constructor calls the four-argument constructor with four 0 values and the two-argument constructor calls the four-argument constructor with two 0 values. As before, the compiler determines which constructor to call, based on the number and the type of arguments.

If present, the invocation of another constructor must be the first line in the constructor.

Class Variables

When a number of objects are created from the same class blueprint, they each have their own distinct copies of *instance variables*. In the case of the Bicycle class, the instance variables are cadence, gear, and speed. Each Bicycle object has its own values for these variables, stored in different memory locations.

Sometimes, you want to have variables that are common to all objects. This is accomplished with the static modifier. Fields that have the static modifier in their declaration are called static *fields* or *class variables*. They are associated with the class, rather than with any object. Every instance of the class shares a class variable, which is in one fixed location in memory. Any object can change the value of a class variable, but class variables can also be manipulated without creating an instance of the class.

For example, suppose you want to create a number of Bicycle objects and assign each a serial number, beginning with 1 for the first object. This ID number is unique to each object and is therefore an instance variable. At the same time, you need a field to keep track of how many Bicycle objects have been created so that you know what ID to assign to the next one. Such a field is not related to any individual object, but to the class as a whole. For this you need a class variable, numberOfBicycles, as follows:

```
public class Bicycle {

    private int cadence;
    private int gear;
    private int speed;

    // add an instance variable for the object ID
    private int id;

    // add a class variable for the
    // number of Bicycle objects instantiated
    private static int numberOfBicycles = 0;

        ...

}
```

Class variables are referenced by the class name itself, as in

Bicycle.numberOfBicycles

This makes it clear that they are class variables.

Constants

The static modifier, in combination with the const modifier, is also used to define constants. The const modifier indicates that the value of this field cannot change.

For example, the following variable declaration defines a constant named pi, whose value is an approximation of pi (the ratio of the circumference of a circle to its diameter):

const double pi = 3.141592653589793;

Summary of Creating and Using Classes and Objects

A class declaration names the class and encloses the class body between braces. The class name can be preceded by modifiers. The class body contains fields, methods, and constructors for the class. A class uses fields to contain state information and uses methods to implement behavior. Constructors that initialize a new instance of a class use the name of the class and look like methods without a return type.

You control access to classes and members in the same way: by using an access modifier such as public in their declaration.

You specify a class variable or a class method by using the static keyword in the member's declaration. A member that is not declared as static is implicitly an instance member. Class variables are shared by all instances of a class and can be accessed through the class name as well as an instance reference.

You create an object from a class by using the new operator and a constructor. The new operator returns a reference to the object that was created. You can assign the reference to a variable or use it directly.

Instance variables - and methods that are accessible to code outside of the class that they are declared in - can be referred to by using a qualified name. The qualified name of an instance variable looks like this:

objectReference.variableName

The qualified name of a method looks like this:

objectReference.MethodName(argumentList)

or:

objectReference.MethodName()

The garbage collector automatically cleans up unused objects. An object is unused if the program holds no more references to it. You can explicitly drop a reference by setting the variable holding the reference to null.

5.4 Exception Handling

An exception is an event, which occurs during the execution of a program that disrupts the normal flow of the program's instructions.

When an error occurs within a method, the method creates an object and hands it off to the runtime system. The object, called an exception object, contains information about the error, including its type and the state of the program when the error occurred. Creating an exception object and handing it to the runtime system is called throwing an exception. After a method throws an exception, the runtime system attempts to find something to handle it. The code to handle this exception is what we provide.

To catch an exception we first put the code which we suspect to throw an error into a try block like

```
Try
{
 if (uIUsername_showEdit.Text = "Test")
   Console.WriteLine("Login Test pass");
 else
   Console.WriteLine("Login Test fail");
}
catch(Exception e)
{
   Console.WriteLine(e.StackTrace);
}
```

Followed by a catch block of code where we tell the system what should be done when the exception occurs. Generally this is where we display the message of the exception object so that we know which exception has occurred and why.

Multiple catch Blocks

A try block can be followed by multiple catch blocks. The syntax for multiple catch blocks looks like the following:

```
try
{
  //Protected code
```

```
}catch(ExceptionType1 e1)

{

   //Catch block

}catch(ExceptionType2 e2)

{

   //Catch block

}catch(ExceptionType3 e3)

{

   //Catch block

}
```

The previous statements demonstrate three catch blocks, but you can have any number of them after a single try. If an exception occurs in the protected code, the exception is thrown to the first catch block in the list. If the data type of the exception thrown matches ExceptionType1, it gets caught there. If not, the exception passes down to the second catch statement. This continues until the exception either is caught or falls through all catches, in which case the current method stops execution and the exception is thrown down to the previous method on the call stack.

Example

Here is a segment of code showing how to use multiple try/catch statements.

```
Try

{

   file = new FileStream(fileName);

   x = (byte) file.read();

}catch(IOException i)

{

Console.WriteLine(i.StackTrace());

   return -1;

}catch(FileNotFoundException f) //Not valid!

{

Console.WriteLine(f.StackTrace());

   return -1;

}
```

The throws/throw Keywords:

If a method does not handle a checked exception, you can throw an exception, either a newly instantiated one or an exception that you just caught, by using the throw keyword. Let us try to understand the difference in throws and throw keywords.

The following method *throw ArgumentNullException.* Since the exception is not handled from within the code, we are using throw keyword to *throw*ArgumentNullException.

```
public class className
{
static void ThrowTest(string value)
    {
        // Generate new exception.
        if (value == null)
        {
            throw new ArgumentNullException("value");
        }
    }
    //Remainder of class definition
}
```

Note: Please refer to this link for more detailed tutorials on C# Language (https://msdn.microsoft.com/en-AU/library/aa288436(v=vs.71).aspx)

ও

6.

Creating a Coded UI Test

Introduction

Many times, functional testers believe that we need to write programs to automate applications. This is not entirely true. Most of the automation tools come with record/replay features which allow you to record user actions and replay those actions back without writing a single line of program. Yes, you might need to make some enhancements to your script, which again can be accomplished without any programming.

In Coded UI we can perform record/replay and automate test cases using Coded UI Test Builder. Coded UI Test Builder is an easy-to-use interface provided by Visual Studio and is generally a quick and efficient way to develop test cases. This chapter is all about understanding the features of Coded UI and how to use them effectively.

Example

As a consultant we have to perform automation feasibility studies across various client applications. The simplest way to do the feasibility study using Coded UI is by using Coded UI Test Builder. By recording and replaying back a basic script we can figure out if the application can be automated using Coded UI. If yes, then we can delve into the bigger effort of configuring a framework in Coded UI.

In this chapter we will define how to record a basic script, replay the script, and save the script using Coded UI Test Builder.

Key objectives:

- Understand Coded UI Test Builder
- Record a basic script
- Replay the script
- Save the script

6.1 Coded UI Test Builder

1. Open Microsoft Visual Studio and create a new project. From the main menu select **File→ New →Project.**

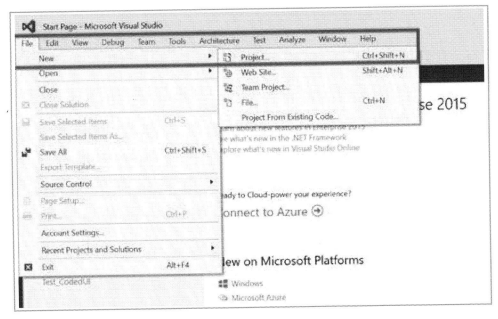

Figure 6.1 – Create a new Project

2. The **Add New Project** dialog box appears.In the **Installed** pane, expand **Visual C#**, and then select **Test**.

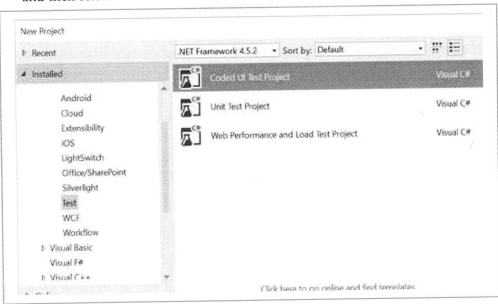

Figure 6.2 – Select Coded UI Test Project

3. In the middle pane, select the **Coded UI Test Project** template (as shown above).

4. In the project name text box enter 'MyFirstScript'.

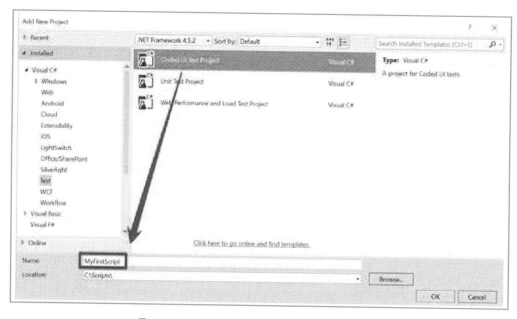

Figure 6.3 – Provide a name to your project

5. Click the **OK** button.

6. The **Generate Code for Coded UI Test** dialog box appears.

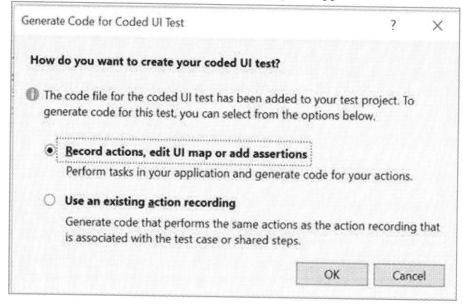

Figure 6.4 – Generating code for Coded UI Test Project

7. Select the **Record actions, edit UI map or add assertions** option and click **OK**.

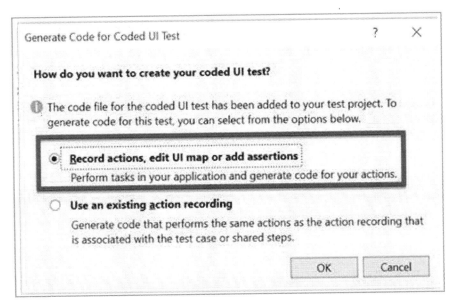

Figure 6.5 – Recording actions in Coded UI

8. The UIMap – Coded UI Test Builder appears on the bottom right side of the screen, and the Visual Studio window is minimized.

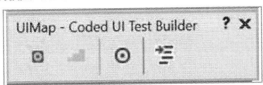

Figure 6.6 – Coded UI Test Builder Toolbar

6.2 Using the Recorder Controls

Alright! Let us record our first script now.

> **Note:** Many first-time users begin by recording a test case from their interactions with a website. When Coded UI Test Builder is first opened, the record button is OFF by default.

Recording your First Test Case

1. Click on the **record** button.

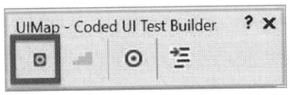

Figure 6.7 – Record button in Coded UI Test Builder Toolbar

2. Open IE browser.

3. Enter the URL for the site you want to test. Let's take our sample application http://www.adactin.com/HotelApp/

4. Assuming the application is already open in IE browser with login page visible, perform the following steps:

   a. Login (Use the username/password with which you have registered earlier).

   b. Search for Hotel.

      i. Select a location, e.g., Sydney

      ii. Select number of rooms, e.g., 2-Two

      iii. Select adults per rooms, e.g., 2-Two

      iv. Click the Search button

   e. Select a Hotel.

      i. Select one of the Hotel Radio buttons, e.g., select radio button next to Hotel Creek.

   d. Book a Hotel.

      i. Enter First Name

      ii. Enter Last Name

      iii. Enter Billing Address

      iv. Enter 16-digit Credit Card no:

      v. Select Credit Card type

      vi. Select Expiry Month

      vii. Select Expiry Year

      viii. Enter CVV number

      ix. Click the Book Now button

   e. After you see the Booking confirmation page, click on the Logout link in the top right corner

   f. Click on the "Click here to Login again" link to go back to the Home page.

5. Pause recording by clicking on the **Pause Recording** button in the record toolbar.

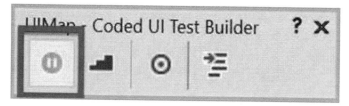

Figure 6.8 - Pause button in Coded UI Test Builder Toolbar

6. Click on the Add and Generate code button.

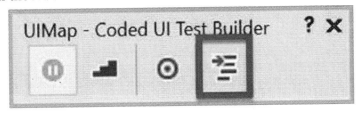

Figure 6.9 – Add and Generate Code button in Coded UI Test Builder Toolbar

7. Clicking on the Add and Generate button will open a window asking for the method name for the script. The default method name is 'RecordedMethod1'

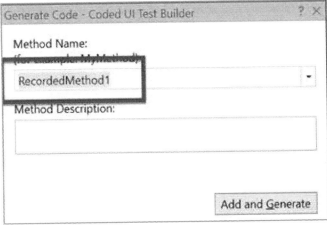

Figure 6.10 – Provide your method name in Coded UI Test Builder Toolbar

8. Change the method name to 'MyFirstScript' and click on the '**Add and Generate**' button.

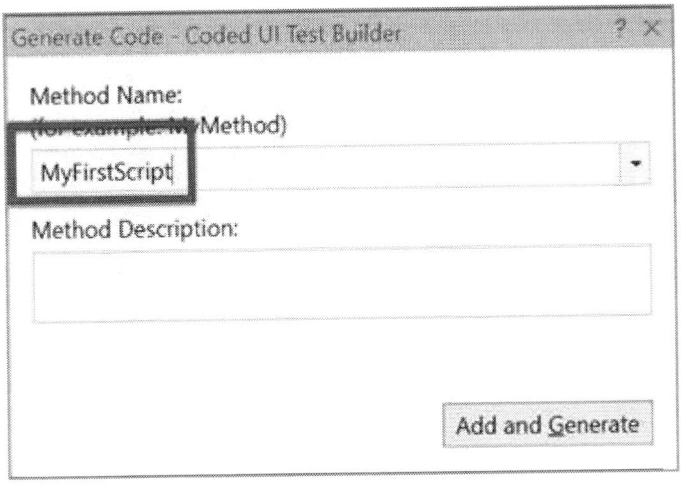

Figure 6.11 - Record button in Coded UI Test Builder Toolbar

9. Close the Coded UI Builder. Go to Visual Studio project. Observe the method name 'MyFirstScript' in the code.

```
[TestMethod]
  0 | 0 references
public void CodedUITestMethod1()
{

    this.UIMap.MyFirstScript();
    // To generate code for this test,

}
```

Figure 6.12 – View the recorded script

Note: Note that only the method name is visible and not the steps. To view the steps we will move into the function 'MyFirstScript'.

10. Right-click on the method name 'MyFirstScript' and click on 'Go To Definition'.

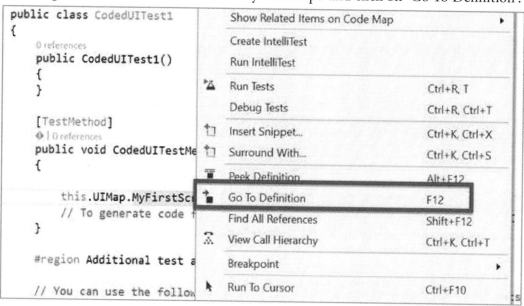

Figure 6.13 – View details of recorded method

11. The UIMap.Designer.cs file opens up which contains code for the method recorded.

```
public void MyFirstScript()
{
    #region Variable Declarations
    HtmlEdit uIUsernameEdit = this.UIAd
    HtmlEdit uIPasswordEdit = this.UIAd
    HtmlInputButton uILoginButton = thi
    HtmlComboBox uILocationComboBox = t
    HtmlComboBox uIRoom_nosComboBox = t
    HtmlComboBox uIChild_roomComboBox =
    HtmlInputButton uISearchButton = th
```

Figure 6.14– Looking at the designer file

During recording, Coded UI Test Builder will automatically insert commands into your method based on your actions. Typically, this will include:

- clicking a Web element like a button or link - *Mouse.Click*

- entering values – *TextBox.Edit*

- selecting options from a drop-down list box - *ComboBox.SelectedItem*

- clicking checkboxes or radio buttons –RadioButton.Selected

6.3 Editing your First Script

Before running our script, we need to edit our script to ensure that the test run executes successfully. As you must have observed that there was a time lag when we clicked on the Login button in our Hotel App application. We need to add this lag in our script recorded above. To do this, perform the following steps -

1. Open Coded UI Project Visual Studio. View the Solution Explorer on the right hand side.

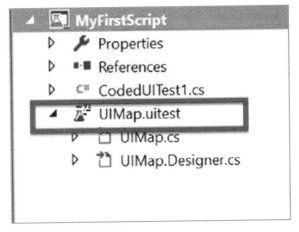

Figure 6.15 – View Solution Explorer

2. There is a file named UIMap.uitest in solution explorer. Double-click on that file.

3. Double-clicking the file will take you to the recorded steps as shown below –

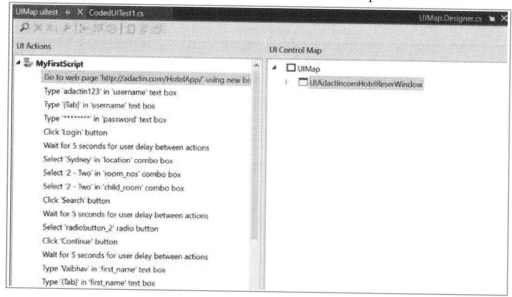

Figure 6.16 – UIMap of recorded script

4. Right-click on the first step and click on properties.

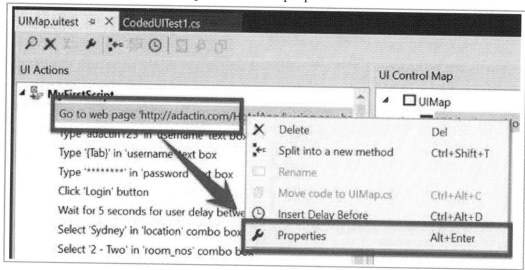

Figure 6.17 – Properties of a recorded step

5. In the properties window change the value of *New Instance* to 'True'.

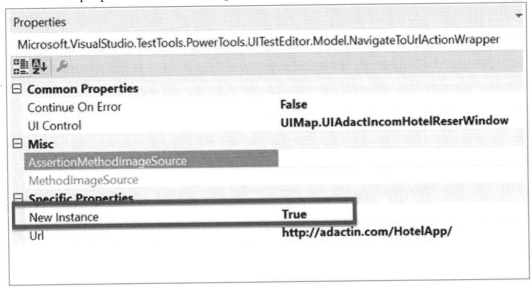

Figure 6.18 – Properties window of recorded step

6. Right-click on the step *Select 'Sydney' in 'location' combo-box*. Click on the option 'Insert Delay Before'.

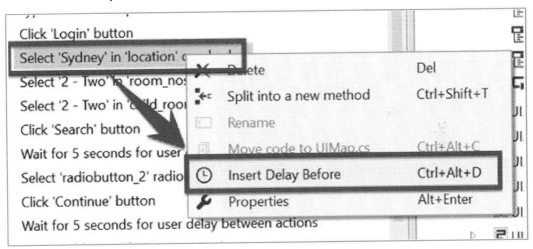

Figure 6.19 – Adding delay between steps

7. Clicking on 'Insert Delay Before' opens up the properties window. Change the value of Delay from 1000 milliseconds to 5000 milliseconds.

> **Note:** Changing delay is an optional step. This is done if your script terminates without executing the test steps. This happens in latest combination of Windows operating system with IE 11.

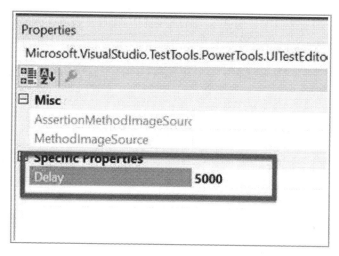

Figure 6.20 – Changing delay from properties window

8. Increase the delay for step *Select 'radiobutton_2' radio button* to 5000 milliseconds.

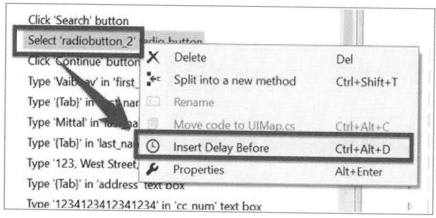

Figure 6.21 – Inserting delay before a recorded step

9. Increase the delay for step *Type 'Vaibhav' in first name text box* to 5000 milliseconds.

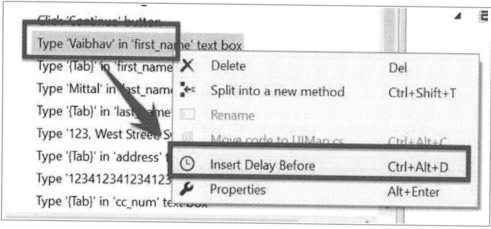

Figure 6.22 - Inserting delay before a recorded step

10. Increase the delay for step *Click 'Logout' button* to 5000 milliseconds.

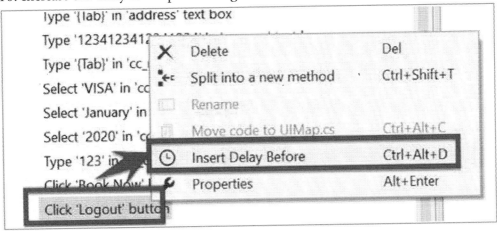

Figure 6.23 - Inserting delay before a recorded step

11. Save the project by clicking on the Save All icon or by pressing Ctrl+Shift+S

Figure 6.24 – Save all files

6.4 Running the test

1. To execute a test, click 'Test' on the main menu and then move to **Test →Run→All Tests**.

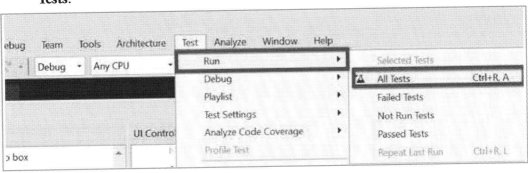

Figure 6.25 – Execute the recorded script

The build mechanism of Visual Studio will start and you will find your test being executed in an Internet Explorer browser.

After the test finishes the execution, you will see the result in Visual Studio.

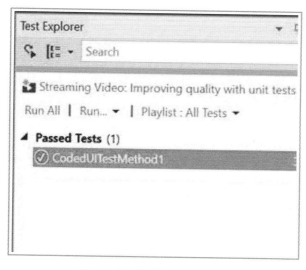

Figure 6.26 – View Results

7.

UI Map

Introduction

In Chapter 6 we recorded a sample script and replayed it. You may be wondering how Microsoft Coded UI actually replayed the whole script. How could it identify the location field and enter the value that we had recorded earlier? Was it like a video recording that got replayed? In this chapter we will understand test automation fundamentals of how a recorded script is replayed and how automation tools recognize objects in the application.

In this chapter we will see

- Understanding Object Recognition fundamentals and how Microsoft Coded UI replays
- Simplification of Web Controls in Coded UI test
- Locate the elements on web page
- What is UI Map?
- UI Map Properties and UI Map Editor
- Working with Objects/Controls using UIMap

7.1 How Does Coded UI Replay Scripts?

Let us take a simple example:

Assume that you parked your car on some level of a big shopping mall before going to a party. For the sake of this example, say you had too many drinks at the party and so took a cab to get home. Next morning, you come back to the mall to pick up your car but you do not remember the location of the car apart from knowing the level on which your car was parked. How will you find your car? Assume that you do not have a remote control for the car!

Figure 7-1 – Sample Car

If we were to find your car, we would go looking for it in the first row and look for the Make and Colour of the car. If we find a car with the same make and colour, then we will go closer to try to identify the car based on the registration number. If all three of the properties match, then we can be sure we will find your car. So the three properties we will look for will be:

- Make of the car
- Colour of the car
- Registration No. of the car

We do not really need to care about height, width or any other details about the car.

This is what the Coded UI tool does and as a matter of fact, this principle is followed by all other automation tools available in the market. They use some key properties of the objects to identify the user interface controls and then use those properties to identify the objects. For instance, if the user clicks on a button, Coded UI uses the label of the button to identify the object.

So this is the process of how Coded UI replays a script:

- While recording, Coded UI stores object property information in the **UI Map. Designer.cs** file in the script
- When we replay the script, Coded UI will pick up the Object properties and try to find the object in the application by matching properties
- Once it finds the object, it will perform the operation (click, select, etc.) on that object

This is the basic automation fundamental required to understand how functional automation tools work. The key point to remember is that the Coded UI script is not a video recording of functionality, but a step by step execution of actions recorded in the script.

7.2 Simplification of Web Controls in Coded UI test

Coded UI test allows the user to capture actions and generates property validations on the controls in the application. In order to do functional testing on the application, Coded UI test needs to playback all the actions that are captured and perform validations on the UI objects in the application interface. So, **Search for controls** forms the base for all the actions and validations done by Coded UI tests.

In order to find the controls in the test execution phase, Coded UI test captures a set of properties on the controls and names them "**Search Properties**" and "**Filter Properties**". Each instance of these is a Name-value pair, with Name being the Property-Name and Value being the actual value of the property during the time of the capture.

Let us take an example. Open project **MyFirstScript**. In this project double-click the file **UIMap.Designer.cs**. The designer file contains properties of all the recorded elements. For this example, we will use the **Login** button properties. The UIMap.Designer.cs file is displayed below –

```
#region Search Criteria


this.mUILoginButton.SearchProperties[HtmlButton.PropertyNames.Id] = "login";

this.mUILoginButton.SearchProperties[HtmlButton.PropertyNames.Name] = "login";

this.mUILoginButton.FilterProperties[HtmlButton.PropertyNames.DisplayText]    =
"Login";

this.mUILoginButton.FilterProperties[HtmlButton.PropertyNames.Type] = "submit";

this.mUILoginButton.FilterProperties[HtmlButton.PropertyNames.Title] = null;

this.mUILoginButton.FilterProperties[HtmlButton.PropertyNames.Class]    =    "login_
button";

this.mUILoginButton.FilterProperties[HtmlButton.PropertyNames.ControlDefinition]    =
"name=\"login\" class=\"login_button\" id=\"lo";

this.mUILoginButton.FilterProperties[HtmlButton.PropertyNames.TagInstance] = "3";

this.mUILoginButton.WindowTitles.Add("AdactIn.com - Hotel Reservation System");


#endregion
```

Table **7.1** – View properties of recorded UI Controls

From the code above, we will be able to get all the properties that are associated with the Login HTML Button control (mUILoginButton).

> **Note:** Search in Coded UI test is a **Breadth-First** which compares each of the controls in the traversal for the match of the properties given in the code.

The first pass of the Search is done for the match of **'All'** properties given in the **SearchProperties** list. Basically this can be referred to as the **AND Condition** of the search properties. In cases, where the results of the search using **SearchProperties** finds exactly one control or doesn't find any control, Coded UI test skips using the **Filter Properties** (even if they are defined in the code) because of the 2 cases,

1. There is exactly one control, so there is no need to apply filters.

2. There are no controls to apply filters.

But, in cases where the list of SearchProperties is not good enough to find the exact control, Coded UI test uses the **filter properties** (one by one) till it finds one exact match. Basically this can be referred to as **Ordered Match.**

In remote cases where Search using FilterProperties also results in more than one control, the **First match** is returned as the resultant control.

7.3 Locate the elements on the web page

Every Web page is nothing but a set of different UI Web elements or objects. Before we work with an element on a page, we need Coded UI to locate that element. The element on the Web page can be located by various locator types. We saw in the previous section that Coded UI automatically identifies the web controls based on their properties and adds them to the **UIMap.designer.cs** class.

To understand the various locators one needs to have a basic understanding of HTML. *Id, name, input, type*, etc., are the HTML tags/attributes. Using these HTML tags, search attributes for a web control can be constructed. We can use these tags or attributes to identify elements.

Let us follow these steps to understand tags and locators.

1. Launch Sample Application URL www.adactin.com/HotelApp in Internet Explorer.

2. Right-click on the **Login** button and select **Inspect element.**

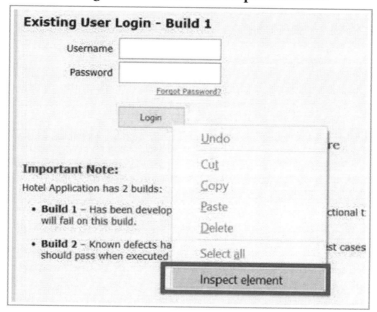

Figure 7.2 – Inspecting UI element in browser

3. You will see below source code

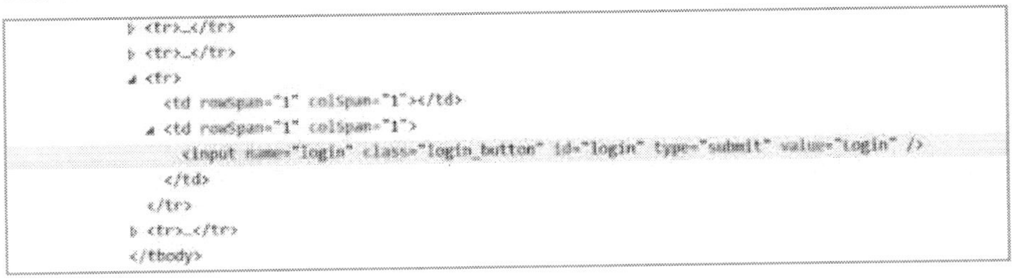

Figure 7.3 – View properties of UI element in web browser

The above source code is HTML based with tags: **input**, **name**, **class**, type which are used to define and identify elements.

4. Now, compare this HTML with the recorded properties of the **Login** button in **UIMap.designer.cs**. The code below has the elements properties highlighted as compared to HTML.

```
#region Search Criteria


this.mUILoginButton.SearchProperties[HtmlButton.PropertyNames.Id] = "login";

this.mUILoginButton.SearchProperties[HtmlButton.PropertyNames.Name] = "login";

this.mUILoginButton.FilterProperties[HtmlButton.PropertyNames.DisplayText]        =
"Login";

this.mUILoginButton.FilterProperties[HtmlButton.PropertyNames.Type] = "submit";

this.mUILoginButton.FilterProperties[HtmlButton.PropertyNames.Title] = null;

this.mUILoginButton.FilterProperties[HtmlButton.PropertyNames.Class]       =       "login_
button";

this.mUILoginButton.FilterProperties[HtmlButton.PropertyNames.ControlDefinition]      =
"name=\"login\" class=\"login_button\" id=\"lo";

this.mUILoginButton.FilterProperties[HtmlButton.PropertyNames.TagInstance] = "3";

this.mUILoginButton.WindowTitles.Add("AdactIn.com - Hotel Reservation System");


#endregion
```

Table 7.2 – Properties of Login button in Coded UI script

The above observation depicts that if required, we can manually extract the properties of an element and add them to the Coded UI script. We will see in the next section how to add an element to our script without recording that element.

7.4 What is UI MAP?

UI Map in Coded UI consists of three files UIMap.cs, UIMap.Designer.cs and UIMap.uitest. These files can be located at the physical location (C:\Scripts\MyFirstScript) where your code resides. The files would Look like below –

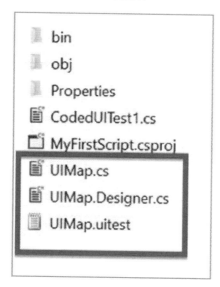

Figure 7.4 – UIMap files in Solution Explorer

UIMap.cs

This is an empty file in your first project. If you want to customize your recorded steps, you can move your code to this file. This is depicted in chapter 9.1. You will then be able to add/edit code as per your specific needs.

By default, this file contains a partial UIMap class that has no methods or properties. All the custom code created will be added to this class.

UIMap.Designer.cs

The UIMap.Designer.cs file contains the code that is generated by the Coded UI Builder to reproduce the structure of the test and provide the connection to the testing framework.

Coded UI Test Builder creates this file when a test is created and automatically re-creates the file each time the test changes thereby allowing the file to be indirectly changed when direct updates are not permitted.

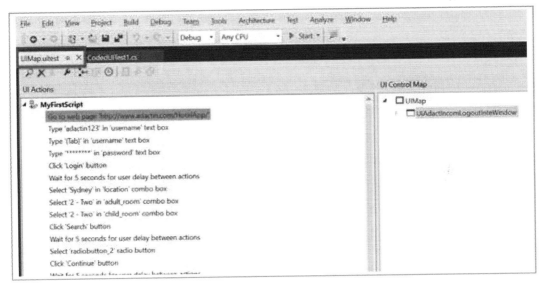

Figure 7.5 – Designer file

UIMap.uitest

This is an XML file that represents the structure of the coded UI test recording and all of its parts. These include the actions and the classes in addition to the methods and properties of those classes. In Visual Studio this file opens up like below -

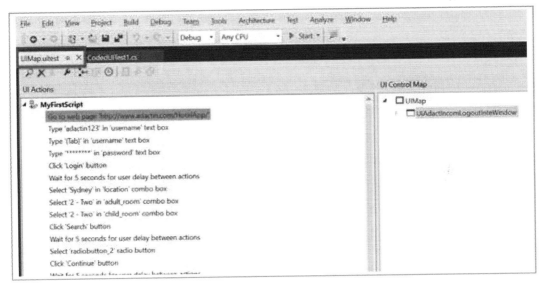

Figure 7.6 – UIMap file showing recorded steps

To view this file in xml format, go to the physical file location and open the uimap.uitest file in notepad. The file would then look like –

Figure 7.7 – XML format of UIMap file

The UIMap.uitest file is not directly editable. However, you can use the Coded UI Builder to modify the test, which automatically modifies the UIMap.uitest file and the UIMap.Designer.cs file.

7.5 UI Map Properties and UI Map editor

UIMap properties

UIMap creates properties for all the recorded elements. The code is auto generated and resides in the designer file. Let us observe a piece of code from the designer file. The following code for the 'Login' button was generated automatically after recording.

A private local HtmlInputButton type variable is created to contain the 'Login' button recorded by Coded UI.

This is shown below –

```
private HtmlInputButton mUILoginButton;
```

This variable (mUILoginButton) is initialized below –

```
public HtmlInputButton UILoginButton

    {

get

        {

if ((this.mUILoginButton == null))

            {

this.mUILoginButton = new HtmlInputButton(this);

#region Search Criteria

this.mUILoginButton.SearchProperties[HtmlButton.PropertyNames.Id] = "login";

this.mUILoginButton.SearchProperties[HtmlButton.PropertyNames.Name]        =
"login";

this.mUILoginButton.FilterProperties[HtmlButton.PropertyNames.DisplayText]        =
"Login";

this.mUILoginButton.FilterProperties[HtmlButton.PropertyNames.Type] = "submit";

this.mUILoginButton.FilterProperties[HtmlButton.PropertyNames.Title] = null;

this.mUILoginButton.FilterProperties[HtmlButton.PropertyNames.Class] = "login_
button";

this.mUILoginButton.FilterProperties[HtmlButton.PropertyNames.
ControlDefinition] = "name=\"login\" class=\"login_button\" id=\"lo";

this.mUILoginButton.FilterProperties[HtmlButton.PropertyNames.TagInstance]        =
"3";

this.mUILoginButton.WindowTitles.Add("AdactIn.com    -    Hotel    Reservation
System");

#endregion

            }

return this.mUILoginButton;

        }

    }
```

Table 7.3 – Code of a recorded button in designer file

UI Map Editor

To open the UI Map editor we go to the Solution Explorer pane in Visual Studio, right-click on UIMap.uitest and click 'Open'.

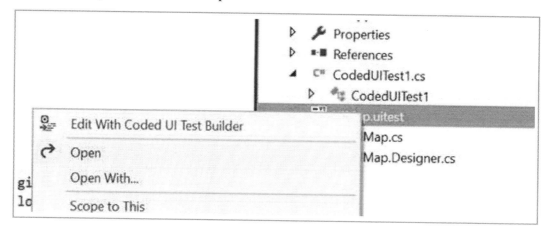

Figure 7.8 – Open UIMap editor file

This will open up the UI Map editor. The UI Code editor contains all of the recorded steps.

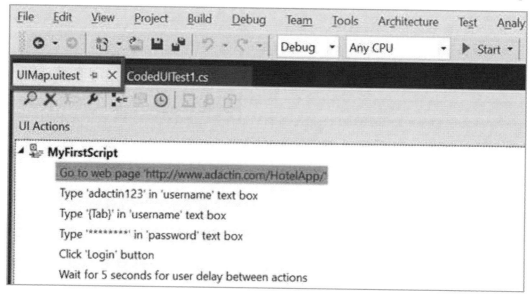

Figure 7.9 – UIMap.uitest file

Using the Coded UI Test Editor is quicker and more efficient than editing the code in your coded UI test methods using the Code Editor. With the Coded UI Test Editor, you can use the toolbar and shortcut menus to quickly locate and modify property values associated with UI actions and controls. For example, you can use the Coded UI Test Editor's toolbar to perform the following commands:

Figure 7.10 – Toolbar on the UIMap editor file

Find helps you locate UI actions and controls.

Delete removes unwanted UI actions.

Rename changes the names for test methods and controls.

Properties opens the Properties Window for selected item.

Split into a new method lets you modularize the UI actions.

Move Code adds custom code to your test methods.

Insert Delay Before adds a pause prior to a UI action, specified in milliseconds.

Locate the UI Control identifies the location of the control in the UI of the application under test.

Locate All helps you verify control property and significant changes to the application's controls.

Copy to clipboard

7.6 Working with Objects/Controls using UIMap

Using the Coded UI Test Editor, you can quickly locate and view all of the UI actions in your test methods. When you select the UI action in the editor, the corresponding control is automatically highlighted. Likewise, if you select a control, the associated UI actions are highlighted. When you select either a UI action or a control, it is then easy to use the Properties window to modify the properties that correspond with it.

Updating action properties

In this section, we will update our recorded script by designing objects using UIMap. If we look at the uimap, we can see the recorded steps are displayed in order. Let us pick up a step where we enter credit card number in the text box.

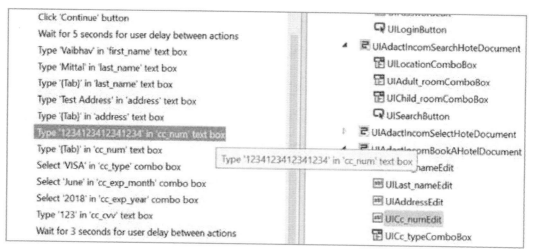

Figure 7.11 – Recorded steps in UIMap file

Let us understand how we can edit the value of this text box without coding or re-recording. We will right-click on this action and select Properties. This will open up the Properties dialog box.

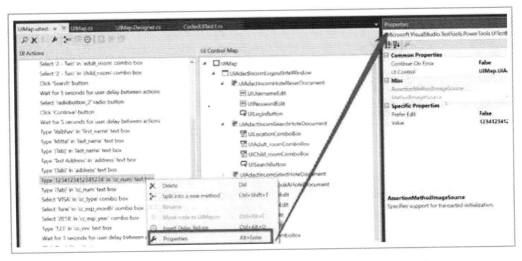

Figure 7.12 – Editing the recorded steps using Properties window

Observe that in the properties dialog box for the credit card text box, we can see the 'value' property has a value of '1234123412341234'. We can modify this value here. Let us change it to '5678567856785678'. Save the project (Ctrl+s). We can see that the new value is reflected in the action under uimap.

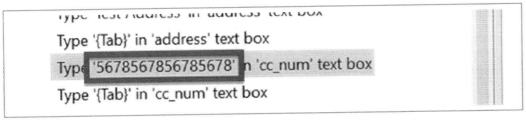

Figure 7.13 – Change the recorded text

Updating control properties

Modifying the properties for a control is done in the same way as the UI actions. In the **UI Control Map** pane, select the control that you want to edit and modify its properties using the Properties window.

Let us take the example of the Login button in our recorded script.

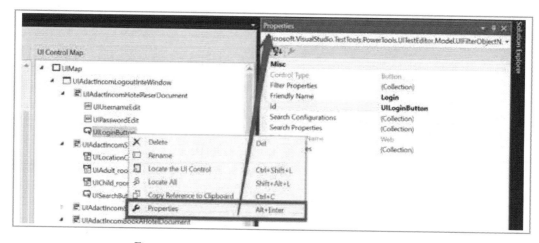

Figure 7.14 – Properties window of Login Button

As an example, a developer might have changed the **(ID)** property on a button control in the source code for the application being tested from "Login" to "idLogin." With the **(ID)** property changed in the application, the coded UI test will not be able to locate the button control and will fail. In this case, the tester can open the **Search Properties** collection and change the **Id** property to match the new value that the developer used in the application. The tester could also change the **Friendly Name** property value from "Login" to "Login Button."

Deleting UI Actions

You can easily remove unwanted UI actions in your coded UI test. In the **UI Action** pane, expand the test method that contains the UI action that you want to delete. Open the shortcut menu for the UI action and choose **Delete**. This is shown below –

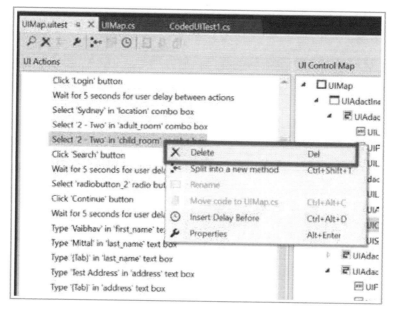

Figure 7.15 – Deleting a recorded step

Split a Test Method

You can split a test method to refine or to modularize the UI actions. For example, your test might have a single test method with UI actions in two container controls. The UI actions might be better modularized in two methods that correspond with one container. In our recorded script we can separate the login functionality with the rest of the script. To achieve that, we can split the script after the login button is clicked. Select the action after clicking the login button. Right-click on this action and select 'Split into a new method'.

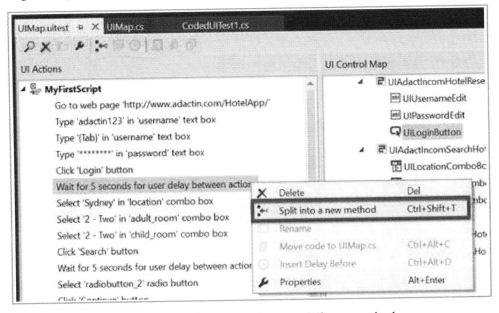

Figure 7.16 – Splitting a script into different methods

Once you split the method into a new one, Visual Studio automatically gives it a name. Deriving from the previous script's name 'MyFirstScript', the new method is named 'MyFirstScript_1'.

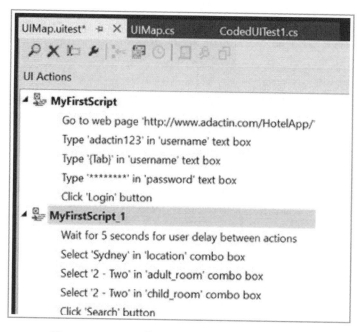

Figure 7.17 – Different methods after splitting

We can now rename both the script names. Click on the script name and press F2. We can rename the script name to 'Login' and 'Booking', respectively. Our UIMap would look like this after these changes –

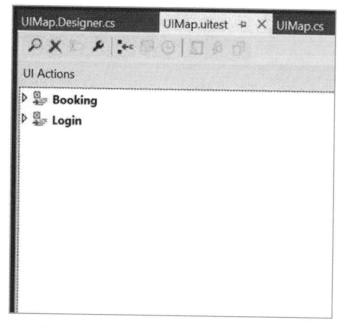

Figure 7.18 – Renaming methods after splitting

If you now try to save and build your solution, you will get an error. Let us try this. Save the solution (Ctrl+Shift+s). Now build the solution (Ctrl+Shift+b). You will observe that the error is –

'UIMap' does not contain a definition for 'MyFirstScript' and no extension method 'MyFirstScript' accepting a first argument of type 'UIMap' could be found (are you missing a using directive or an assembly reference?)

The reason behind this error is that we have changed the name of the script. Therefore codeduitest1.cs class throws this error. When we make changes in UIMap.uitest, these changes are reflected in the designer file automatically. However, we need to make these changes manually in the cs file. We will now open codeduitest1.cs file and make the below changes -

Old code –

```
public void CodedUITestMethod1()

    {

this.UIMap.MyFirstScript();


// To generate code for this test, select "Generate Code for Coded UI Test"
from the shortcut menu and select one of the menu items.

    }
```

Table 7.4 – Method name before splitting

New code –

```
public void CodedUITestMethod1()

    {

this.UIMap.Login();

this.UIMap.Booking();


// To generate code for this test, select "Generate Code for Coded UI Test"
from the shortcut menu and select one of the menu items.

    }
```

Table 7.5 – New methods after splitting in UIMap.uitest file

Locating a UI Control

Sometimes, it can be difficult to visualize where controls are located in the UI of the application under test. One of the capabilities of the coded UI Test Editor is that you can select a control listed in the UI control map and view its location in the application under test. Using the **Locate the UI Control** feature on the application under test can also be used to verify search property modifications you have made to a control.

In the **UI Control Map** pane, select the control that you want to locate in the application associated with the test. Next, open the shortcut menu for the control and then choose **Locate the UI Control**. In the application that is being tested, the control is designated with a blue border. In our example, let us try to locate the 'Login' button.

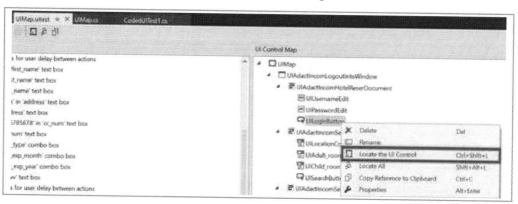

Figure 7.19 – Locate the recorded control on application under test

Before selecting this option, the application under test should be running in the browser. Now select this option. You will see that Coded UI will try to locate this control –

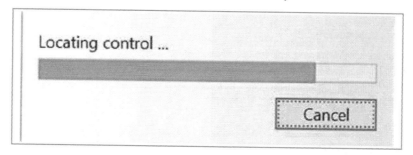

Figure 7.20 – Coded UI trying to locate recorded UI control

After a few seconds, the control is highlighted on the application under test.

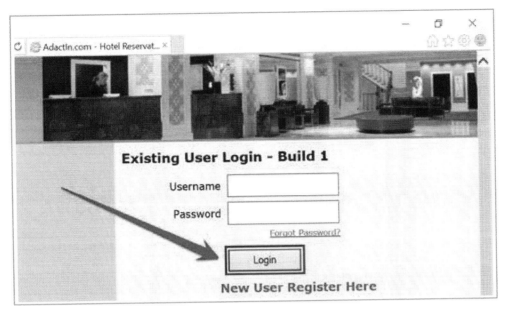

Figure 7.21 – Coded UI successfully located Login Button

Exercise

1. Change the value of the credit card details from UIMap.uitest.

2. Locate other web elements in the UI Control Map.

೧ಌ

Multiple Choice Questions Set-1

1. What are the three main components of Coded UI UIMap?

    A. UIMap.uitest, UIMap.Action.cs, UIMap.cs

    B. UIMap.uitest, UIMap.Designer.cs, UIMap.cs

    C. UIMap.Action.cs, UIMap.Designer.cs, UIMap.cs

    D. UIMap.uitest, UIMap.Designer.cs, UIMap.Action.cs

2. Which of the following browsers supports the record and play feature of Coded UI?

    A. Chrome

    B. Firefox

    C. Internet Explorer

    D. Safari

3. Which of these is a supported language for Coded UI?

    A. Java

    B. C#

    C. Ruby

    D. C++

4. Which of these components is used to record a Coded UI Test?

    A. Properties

    B. Solution Explorer

    C. Test Explorer

    D. Coded UI Test Builder

5. After recording in Coded UI, where can we see the recorded steps?

    A. CodedUITest1.cs

    B. UIMap.uitest

    C. UIMap.cs

    D. Any of the above

6. How do we add delays between recorded steps?

   A. Can be done by hand coding only

   B. Select 'Insert Delay Before' option from context menu

   C. Using shortcut Ctrl+Alt+C

   D. Recording the delay

7. Where can we see the Coded UI project in Visual Studio IDE?

   A. Solution Explorer

   B. Class Explorer

   C. Test Explorer

   D. Any of the above

8. Which window is used to see the test results?

   A. Solution Explorer

   B. Class Explorer

   C. Test Explorer

   D. Any of the above

9. Which file contains the code for recorded Coded UI script?

   A. UIMap.cs

   B. UIMap.Designer.cs

   C. CodedUITest1.cs

   D. None of the above

10. How do you change the recorded value of a text box from 'abc' to 'xyz' within UIMap.uitest?

   A. Use the Properties window of the recorded step

   B. Use hand coding only

   C. Cannot be changed once recorded

Answers

Q1. Answer: B

Explanation – The main components of a Coded UI test are - UIMap.uitest, UIMap.Designer.cs, UIMap.cs

Q2. Answer: C

Explanation – Internet explorer is the default browser supported by Coded UI

Q3. Answer: B

Explanation – Being a Microsoft product Coded UI supports C#

Q4. Answer: D

Explanation – Coded UI Test Builder is the default tool to record scripts in Visual Studio IDE

Q5. Answer: B

Explanation – All the recorded steps can be seen sequentially in the UIMap.uitest file.

Q6. Answer: B

Explanation – Right click on any recorded step in UIMap.uitest file. There is an option 'Insert Delay Before' to add the delay before that step

Q7. Answer: A

Explanation – The Solution Explorer window in Visual Studio shows all the project files

Q8. Answer: C

Explanation –The Test Explorer window shows all the scripts and execution results

Q9. Answer: B

Explanation – The UIMap.Designer.cs file houses all the recorded code. This code is generated automatically by Microsoft Coded UI. This file should not be modified.

Q10. Answer: A

Explanation –Right-click the recorded step. Select Properties. The Properties window contains the recorded value for the text box. This can then be changed.

ɛ๏ɔ

8.

Adding Assertions in Coded UI

Introduction

Till now, we have just executed a set of actions a functional tester will perform. We have not validated the application's functionality by comparing any actual values on the application against expected values.

To accomplish this, we will insert assertion points in Coded UI. In this chapter we will understand the need for assertions and how to insert assertions in Coded UI script. Also we will understand the different kinds of assertions or checks we can perform in Coded UI.

Example

As a consultant, we need to work with lots of assertion in our everyday work, either manually or automatically,both depending on the complexity and time. It is extremely important to design them in advance. Good assertion is necessary; otherwise we risk gathering wrong/ inaccurate information from QA work. This can delay the delivery of software or leave issues uncovered in the product.To write good assertions, we have to examine the part of the software to test carefully, find out what's unique about it, and what we need to find out as a sufficient proof of its working.

In this chapter we will understand the need for assertions and how to add them in a Coded UI script.

Key objectives:

- Need for assertions
- Adding assertion to Coded UI script
- Type of assertions

8.1 Need for Assertions

An assertion point is a specialized step that compares two values and reports the result. An assertion point compares the actual results from the test run, with the expected results in the test case.

A basic test cannot be considered a valid functional test without some form of validation.

You use a checkpoint to:

- Verify the state of an object
- Confirm that an application performs as expected

An assertion checks whether an application responds appropriately when a user performs tasks correctly while testing the application. An assertion can ensure a user is barred from performing certain tasks by confirming invalid or incomplete data are flagged with appropriate messages.

- Examples of validation are: Specifying limits, conditions, or boundaries

Example

We were once testing an investment banking application where we could create varied instruments such as bonds, ADRs, etc. When creating an instrument, we would receive a "Save was successful" message and a unique instrument number. As part of our test case, we had to verify that the "Save was successful" message appears. We also had to verify that we could search using the same instrument number and verify that all details were saved correctly. As part of our automation scripts, we had to verify both these functions, so we used an assertion point to accomplish this.

8.2 Adding an Assertion to a Coded UI script

An assertion can be inserted in the Coded UI script. In this section we will lay out and try to automate a test scenario containing an expected result.

Test Scenario

Let us take a simple test case for automation from our Hotel Application.

Test Objective: To verify that when a location is selected on the Search Hotel page, the same location is displayed on the Select Hotel page

Test Steps:

1. Login to the application using valid User credentials
2. Select "Sydney" from the Location field on the Search Hotel page
3. Keep all the default selections
4. Click the Search Button
5. Verify the correct Location is displayed on the Select Hotel page

Expected Result

1. "Sydney" should appear in the Location column on the Select Hotel search results page

Creating a new project and reusing existing script

To start with a new script, we will follow these steps –

1. We will create a copy of our existing project under the same solution. To create a new project, follow the steps from Chapter 6.

2. Name the project as '**AddAssertions**'.

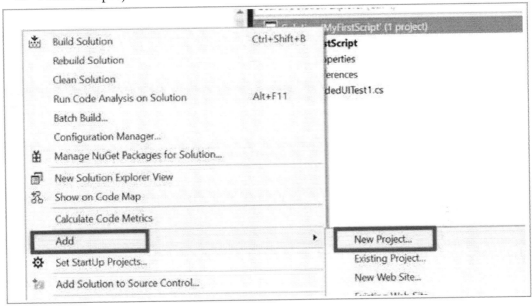

Figure 8.1 – Creating a new Coded UI project

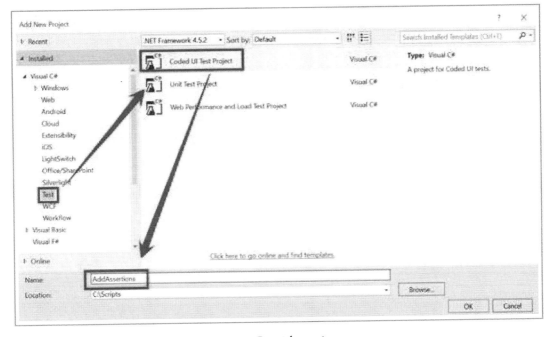

Figure 8.2 – Provide project name

3. In this new project, copy and paste the UIMap.uitest file from the previous project.

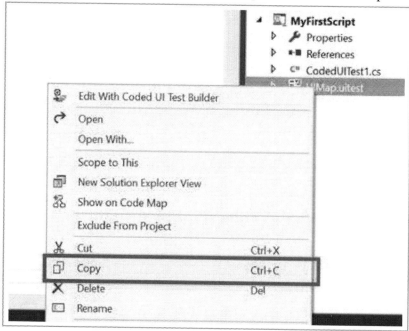

Figure 8.3 – Copy recorded steps from the previous project

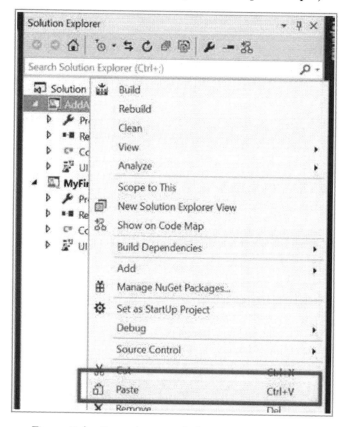

Figure 8.4 – Paste the recorded steps in new project

4. We now need to align the namespace of the UIMap.cs and UIMap.designer.cs file in the 'AddAssertions' project.

5. Open the files **UIMap.cs** and **UIMap.designer.cs** and change the namespace from **MyFirstScript** to **AddAssertions**.

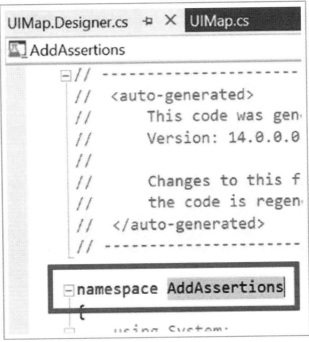

Figure 8.5 – Updating the new project with correct namespace names

6. The new code will need to call the recorded methods in the **CodedUITest1.cs** as well. Open **CodedUITest1.cs** in the **'AddAssertions'** project and add the following code -

```
[TestMethod]

public void CodedUITestMethod1()

    {

this.UIMap.Login();

this.UIMap.Booking();

// To generate code for this test, select "Generate Code for Coded UI Test" from
the shortcut menu and select one of the menu items.

    }
```

Table 8.1 – View existing code in new project

7. Scroll down the file **CodedUITest1.cs** and add the below mentioned code as well –

```
publicUIMap UIMap

        {

get

            {

if ((this.map == null))

                {

this.map = newUIMap();

                }


returnthis.map;

            }

        }


privateUIMap map;
```

Table 8.2 – Code to add in new project

8. Go to **Build→Build Solution** and compile the project.

How to insert a verification point

Let us see how to insert a verification point.

Observe the scenario after logging into the Hotel App website you will reach here –

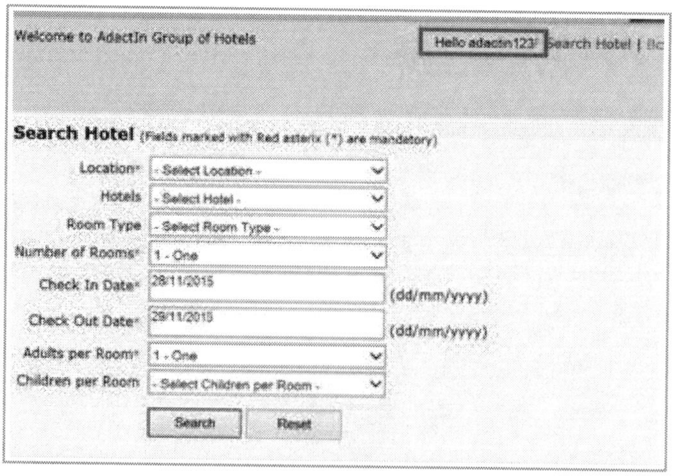

Figure 8.6 – Verification point in HotelApp website

We will now validate if the correct user name is displayed on the website after logging in.

For script purposes, open the Coded UI Test Builder when you reach this page. Do **NOT** click on the record button.

Notice the following button is enabled on the Coded UI Test Builder toolbar –

Figure 8.7 – Coded UI Test Builder Toolbar

This button is used to locate any control on the application under test. We will now see how to use this button to add assertion to a Coded UI test.

1. Click on this control and keep the left mouse button pressed down.
2. Move the mouse pointer to this cell location until it is highlighted.

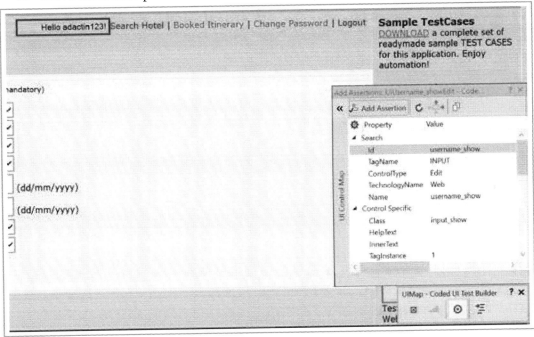

Figure 8.8 – Identify text using Coded UI Test Builder

3. When the cell is highlighted in Blue, release the left mouse button and the Add Assertions window will open and be populated with this control's details.

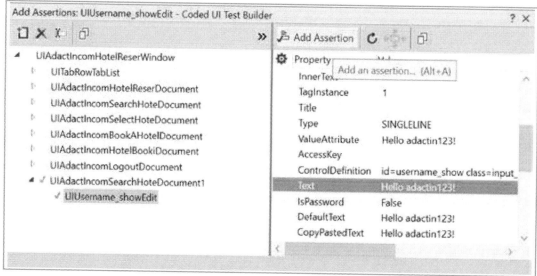

Figure 8.9 – Add assertion using Coded UI Test Builder

4. The above window showcases all the properties of the highlighted control. We will validate the text of this particular control.

5. In the property section scroll down to 'Text' property.

6. Right-click the Text property and select the **Add AssertionLocation** button.

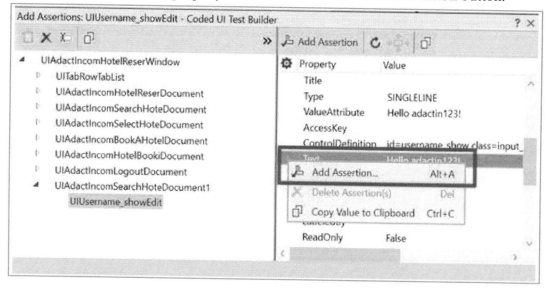

Figure 8.10 – Add Assertion dialog

7. The assertion dialog box will open. This dialog box will contain various options for comparing the selected property with a custom value.

8. In this case we will select the 'AreEqual' comparator to compare the text of the selected control to 'Hello Adactin123!'.

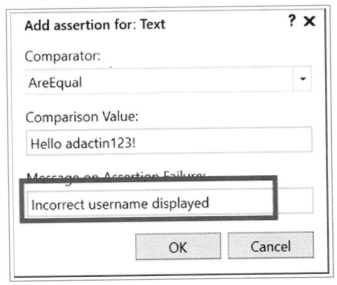

Figure 8.11 – Comparing parameters

9. The dialog box also will prompt for a failure message to be displayed in case of a failure. Click the **OK** button.

10. We will now generate the method name for the same. Let us name it 'MyFirstAssert'.

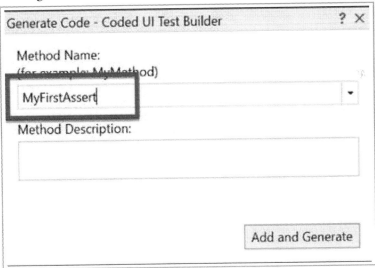

Figure 8.12 – Generate a new method for Assertion script

11. Click the **Add and Generate** button.

12. Now close the Coded UI Test Builder.

13. The focus will now move to the Visual Studio project. In order to execute this code, we have to make some changes to our code.

```
[TestMethod]

public void CodedUITestMethod1 ()

    {

this. UIMap.Login();

this. UIMap.MyFirstAssert();

this. UIMap.Booking();


// To generate code for this test, select "Generate Code for Coded UI
Test" from the shortcut menu and select one of the menu items.

    }
```

Table 8.3 – View updated script with Assertion code

14. Your code is ready to be executed now. To run this specific test and not all the tests in this class, go to menu **Test → Windows → Test Explorer**.

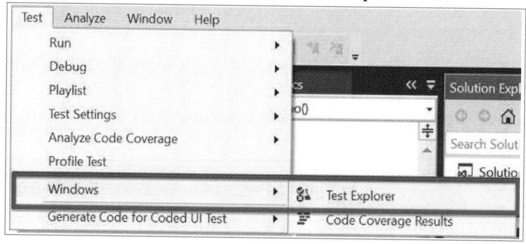

Figure 8.13 – Test Explorer to execute script

15. In the **Test Explorer** window, you can select the test you want to execute. Alternatively, you can do any of the following –

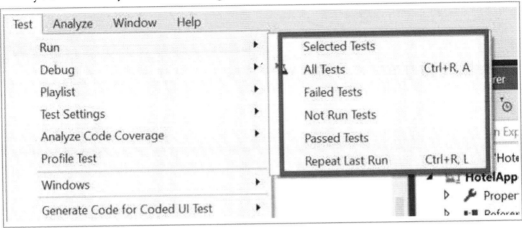

Figure 8.14 – Select your test to run

8.3 Types of Assertions in Visual Studio

In the above example, we used the Assert ***AreEqual.*** However, tthere are many assertions provided by Visual Studio ***Assert*** class. To observe all the methods provided by this class, we need to inspect our function '**MyFirstAssert**' from the code above.

Let us go to the code in our **CodedUITest1.cs** file.

```
[TestMethod]

    public void CodedUITestMethod1 ()

    {

this. UIMap.Login();

this. UIMap.MyFirstAssert();

this. UIMap.Booking();

// To generate code for this test, select "Generate Code for Coded UI Test"
from the shortcut menu and select one of the menu items.

    }
```

Table 8.4 – View the existing script

In this code we will analyse the function '**MyFirstAssert**'. To do that, we will right-click this function and select **Go To Definition**. The short cut for this is the F12 key.

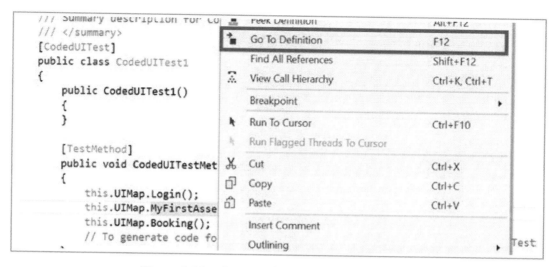

Figure 8.15 – Go to Definition of Assert method

This will take you to the method definition where you will see the following code –

```
public void MyFirstAssert()

    {

#region Variable Declarations

HtmlEdit uIUsername_showEdit = this.
UIAdactIncomHotelReserWindow.
UIAdactIncomSearchHoteDocument1.UIUsername_showEdit;

#endregion

Playback.Wait(5000);

// Verify that the 'Text' property of 'username_show' text box
equals 'Hello adactin123!'

Assert.AreEqual(this.MyFirstAssert1ExpectedValues.
UIUsername_showEditText, uIUsername_showEdit.Text,
"Incorrect username displayed");

    }
```

Table 8.5 – View code of Assert method

Note: We have added some wait for the page to load before the assertion takes place.

Here you will find the usage of the **Assert** class. Move your cursor next to the Assert class and press the Ctrl+Space keys. This is a short-cut for intellisense (Visual Studio feature to predict the word when we are typing the starting letter of the word) which will open up all the method names for the **Assert** class. Your screen should display the methods as shown below –

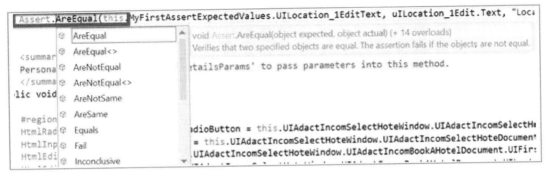

Figure 8.16 – View methods of Assert class

We can select any of these functions based on our assertion requirements. We would be using these classes and functions more when we write custom code in upcoming chapters.

Let us understand some of the most common assertion methods:

- AreEqual
- AreNotEqual
- IsNull
- IsNotNull
- AreSame

AreEqual

This method verifies that two specified objects are equal. The assertion fails if the objects are not equal. It can also display a message if the assertion fails.

AreNotEqual

This method verifies that two specified objects are not equal. The assertion fails if the objects are equal. It can also display a message if the assertion fails.

IsNull

This method verifies that the specified object is **null**. The assertion fails if it is not **null**. It can also display a message if the assertion fails.

IsNotNull

This method verifies that the specified object is not **null**. The assertion fails if it is **null**. It can also display a message if the assertion fails.

AreSame

This method verifies that two specified object variables refer to the same object. The assertion fails if they refer to different objects. It can also display a message if the assertion fails.

StringAssert Class

Apart from the above mentioned methods of the **Assert** class, there is also a **StringAssert** class that provides different methods to be used for string comparisons.

In the *MyFirstAssert* method, write *StringAssert* and type '.' (dot). A list of methods will pop up.

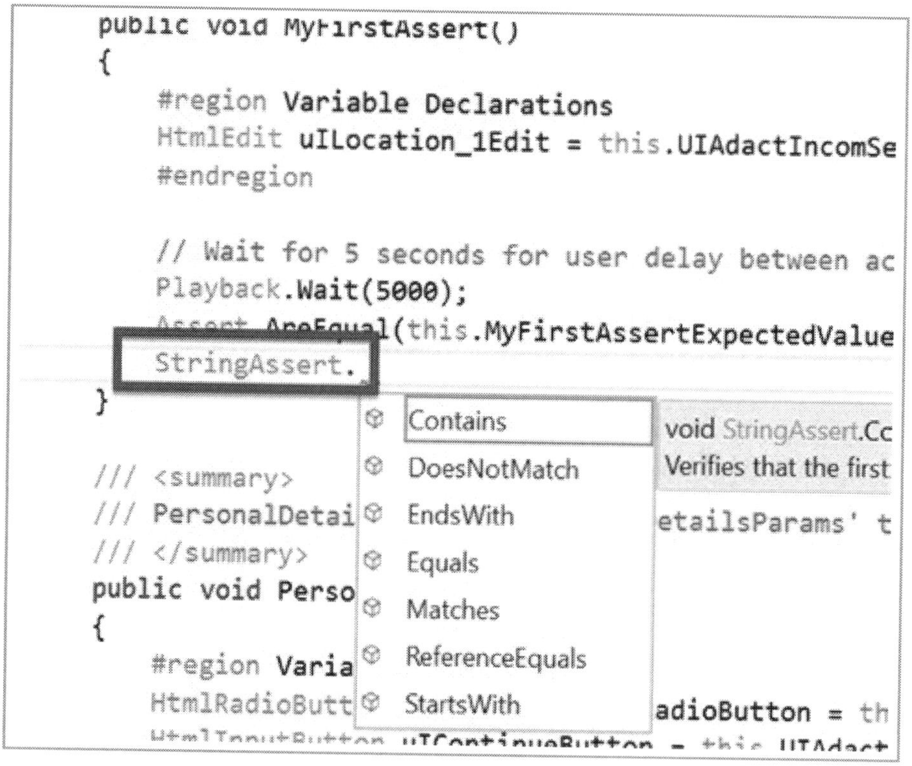

```
public void MyFirstAssert()
{
    #region Variable Declarations
    HtmlEdit uILocation_1Edit = this.UIAdactIncomSe
    #endregion

    // Wait for 5 seconds for user delay between ac
    Playback.Wait(5000);
    Assert.AreEqual(this.MyFirstAssertExpectedValue
    StringAssert.
}                    ┌──────────────────┐
                     │ ⊛ │Contains      │  void StringAssert.Cc
/// <summary>        │ ⊛ │DoesNotMatch  │  Verifies that the first
/// PersonalDetai    │ ⊛ │EndsWith      │  etailsParams' t
/// </summary>       │ ⊛ │Equals        │
public void Perso    │ ⊛ │Matches       │
{                    │ ⊛ │ReferenceEquals│
    #region Varia    │ ⊛ │StartsWith    │  adioButton = th
    HtmlRadioButt    └──────────────────┘
    HtmlInputButton uIContinueButton = this.UIAdact
```

Figure 8.17 – View methods of StringAssert class

This class contains a variety of useful methods such as StringAssert.Contains, StringAssert. Matches, and StringAssert.StartsWith. Some of the important methods and their descriptions are detailed below –

Method Name	Description
Contains(String, String, String)	Verifies that the first string contains the second string. Displays a message if the assertion fails. This method is case sensitive.
EndsWith(String, String, String)	Verifies that the first string ends with the second string. Displays a message if the assertion fails. This method is case sensitive.
Matches(String, Regex, String)	Verifies that the specified string matches the regular expression. Displays a message if the assertion fails.
StartsWith(String, String, String)	Verifies that the first string begins with the second string. Displays a message if the assertion fails. This method is case sensitive.

Table 8.6 – List of StringAssert methods

Note: The methods in the **Assert** and **StringAssert** classes have different overloaded methods. We have mentioned the ones that we will be using in our projects. The same methods also have overloaded methods where we do not need to enter a *failure* string.

Exercise

1. Change the Assert method to *IsNotNull* and execute the script. The script should pass.

൚

9.

Synchronization in Coded UI

Introduction

In any Web automation project, the automation success depends upon the robustness of your scripts; whether that's adaptation of your code to project or software changes, or synchronization of the script with the site's performance.

Many a time, your application performance will vary which will require you to manipulate your WebDriver script's execution speed.

In one of the applications that we tested, it took more than 60 seconds for an application form to save and confirm that save was successful. How does Coded UI support these situations?

Synchronization is a critical issue for any test automation script. You may think that synchronization of test script actions is a built-in ability of today's functional testing tools. Reality shows that many unexpected test script failures are related to synchronization issues generating false negative results. These false negatives make it hard to detect real application problems as each test script failure may be related to a test script synchronization issue. Synchronization errors are timing issues therefore they are non-deterministic, heavily dependent on the HW/SW, the network and their utilization. The biggest challenge in automating a Web application is the loading of a Web page which is always at the mercy of certain conditions, such as:

- Load on the server
- Network speed
- Performance of AUT
- Ajax call to load an element

In this chapter we will learn the concept of synchronization and how it needs to be incorporated in the Coded UI script.

> **Note**: In this chapter, we will start by moving our recorded steps from UIMap.uitest to UIMap.cs. This is our beginning to learn how we can customize our script using hand coding.

Key objectives:

- Move recorded script to C# file for hand coding
- Importance of Synchronization
- Approaches used for Script Synchronization
- Synchronization of Coded UI script

9.1 Move recorded script to C# file for hand coding

We will start by creating a new project under the solution 'MyFirstScript'. Let us follow the same procedure as in the previous chapter. This time we will name the project 'AddSynchronization'.

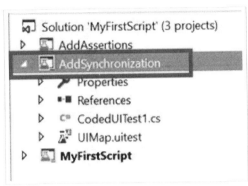

Figure 9.1 – Create a new project

Copy the UIMap.uitest file from the 'AddAssertions' project created in the last chapter. Update the namespace references and CodedUITest1.cs file. The project should now compile successfully.

When you have finished creating the new project, You will have to move the code from the UIMap.uitest file to the UIMap.cs file. Visual Studio provides a one-click action for this activity. Go to UIMap.uitest and highlight the **Login** function. Right-click the Login function and you will see the option to move the code to UIMap.cs.

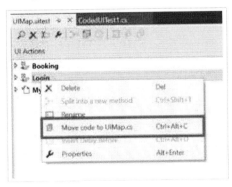

Figure 9.2 – Move the recorded steps in c# file

Move the function 'Login' and 'Booking' to UIMap.cs. The Assert statement cannot be moved to the cs file because it is inherently present in the designer file. After moving the code to the UIMap.cs file, you will observe that this file contains the custom code which references objects and methods within UIMap.Designer.cs.

Note:UIMap.cs is the file where we can add more custom code and assertions.

9.2 Importance of Synchronization

What is script synchronization?

Test scripts need to be synchronized in a way that the script driving the application **waits** until the AUT is ready to accept the next user input.

The following are some situations where synchronization is required:

- The creation of a window (more general control) must be completed before it can receive messages/commands
- A page must be completely loaded before you can click on a link on the page
- A button must be activated before you can click on it
- A data grid must load the row before you can verify the row
- A data grid must be completely loaded before you can verify the row count of the grid
- A tree must be expanded before you can select one of its children
- When selecting a tree node, the details pane [of the node] needs to be completely loaded before you can verify text on it

Ajax specific synchronization problems

Ajax is shorthand for Asynchronous JavaScript and XML. With Ajax, Web applications can retrieve data from the server asynchronously in the background without interfering with the display and behavior of the existing page. The use of Ajax techniques has led to an increase in interactive or dynamic interfaces on Web pages. Data is usually retrieved using the XMLHttpRequest object. The asynchronous nature of Ajax makes it hard to detect when an Ajax request is fulfilled and when the application is ready to proceed with the next UI interaction (as the UI is not blocked during executing the request).

Even worse, the current browsers do not indicate the execution and the end of the execution of Ajax based requests. Processing normal HTML pages is indicated visually by an animated icon in the browser and programmatically by an event that is fired when processing is completed. This means that there is no easy way to decide when the application is ready to process the next UI action. Usually this is not a problem for humans because we have multiple cognitive techniques to detect if an application is ready to proceed. Humans are also not that fast when working with an application compared to "computer programs" like test automation tools that are driving the application. So many of the synchronization problems do not appear when a human is accessing the application. But asynchronous behavior as seen in Ajax applications is a real nightmare for a testing tool.

9.3 Approaches used for Script Synchronization

A major task in automating Web applications is to wait for the HTML element to appear in the page before your automation test code starts performing an action on it. You need to make sure that the Web element is present before the code begins working on it. This can be achieved by waiting for the element to appear in the page. For synchronization we can implement different execution control mechanisms:

1. Playback.Wait()
2. UI Test Control Methods

Playback.Wait()

This method is used implicitly by Visual Studio when we insert a delay using UIMap. uitest. As mentioned in earlier chapters, we can explicitly insert a delay before a test step in UIMap.uitest using the following button -

Insert Delay Before adds a pause prior to a UI action, specified in milliseconds.

This button automatically generates the code. To verify, go back to your project 'AddSynchronization' and you will find the following code in the UIMap.cs file –

```
Playback.Wait(5000);
```

The above code makes the playback pause for a specified time. The duration is specified in brackets. The wait duration is in milliseconds. 5000 milliseconds is equivalent to 5 seconds.

> **Note:** Always use *Playback.Wait()* over *Thread.Sleep()*. *Playback.Wait()*calls [internally] *Thread.Sleep()* in smaller chunks in a for-loop while checking for a user cancel\break operation.

UI Test Control Methods

Visual Studio provides wait methods for implementing a dynamic **explicit** wait. These various methods provide a set of predefined conditions to wait before proceeding further in the code. The following table shows some common conditions that we frequently come across when automating Web browsers supported by these methods:

UI Test Control methods	Detail
WaitForControlReady	Waits for the control to be ready to accept mouse and keyboard input. The engine implicitly calls this API for all actions to wait for the control to be ready before doing any operation.
WaitForControlEnabled	Waits for the control to be enabled when the wizard is doing some asynchronous validation of the input by making calls to the server.
WaitForControlExist	Waits for the control to appear on the UI. For example, you are expecting an error dialog after the application has done the validation of the parameters. The time taken for validation is variable. You can use this method to wait for the error dialog box.
WaitForControlNotExist	Waits for the control to disappear from the UI. For example, you can wait for the progress bar to disappear.
WaitForControlPropertyEqual	Waits for the specified property of the control to have the given value. For example, you wait for the button text to change to 'Logout'.
WaitForControlPropertyNotEqual	Waits for the specified property of the control to have the opposite of a specified value. For example, you wait for the edit box to be not read-only, that is, editable.
WaitForControlCondition	Waits for the specified predicate to be **true**. This can be used for complex wait operation (like OR conditions) on a given control.
WaitForCondition<T>	All the previous methods are instance methods of UI Test Control. This method is a static method. This method also waits for the specified predicate to be **true** but it can be used for complex wait operation (like OR conditions) on multiple controls.

Table 9.1 – UI Test Control methods

Note: More details on these methods can be found at the link -https://msdn.microsoft.com/en-us/library/gg131072.aspx

9.4 Synchronization of Coded UI Script

Let us take a practical scenario to illustrate script synchronization.

Problem Description – As part of our Hotel booking workflow, when a user clicks on **Book Now** an order number is generated. We need to write this order number in the result.

The challenge here is that when a user clicks on the 'Book Now' button it takes approximately 6-8 seconds before the order number is generated. So to resolve this we need script synchronization.

Solution – We can follow multiple solutions to this problem.

Use Static Wait, which is the easiest and simplest of all, before you fetch the value from the order number field

- Use Explicit Wait to wait for the existence of the Logout Button. The Logout button only appears after the order number has been generated.

Let us look at the existing code and figure out the current behaviour. Open the UIMap.cs file and find the code when we click the 'Book Now' button.

```
// Click 'Book Now' button
Mouse.Click(uIBookNowButton, newPoint(130, 17));


// Wait for 5 seconds for user delay between actions
Playback.Wait(5000);


// Click 'Logout' button
Mouse.Click(uILogoutButton, newPoint(63, 23));
```

Table 9.2 – Observe the Wait command

Observe that we are waiting for 5 seconds after clicking the 'Book Now' button.

Note: The only drawback of the above process is that the system will wait all 5 seconds even though the actual order insertion might take only 3-4 seconds.

Let us edit our code to apply the UI Test Control methods discussed above. For this scenario, we will need to first identify the booking order number control (text box) on the webpage and in our script.

Adding new control to UI Control Map

Let us understand how to capture a new control that we have **not** recorded in our existing script. In this scenario we would like to add the Booking order number when a user books a hotel on the Adactin website (AUT).

Figure 9.3 – Order number field in HotelApp website

1. To record/add this control to our project, we will initiate the **Coded UI Test Builder** again.

2. We will then highlight this text box using the locator button. Locate this text box as shown below –

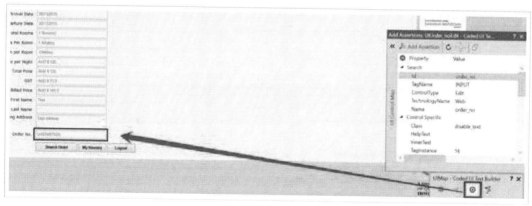

Figure 9.4 – Recording Order number text box using Coded UI Test Builder

3. When the text box is identified, the next step is to add this control to our existing project. To do that, we will use the **Add Control to UI Control Map** button on the control identifier used above. This button is depicted in the image below –

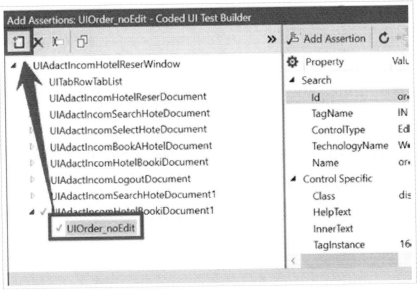

Figure 9.5 – Adding new UI Control

4. Once the required control is identified, we will click the button above and the control will be added to the existing Control Map.

5. Now we just need to generate the code for the same. To do that click the Generate Code button and leave the Method Name blank/empty.

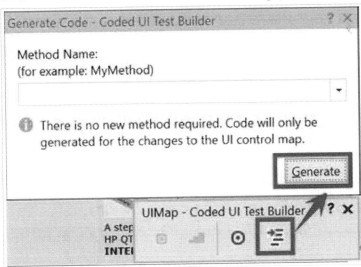

Figure 9.6 – Generating steps and appending to existing script

6. This will push the control to our project. Now close the Coded UI Test Builder.

7. Go to UIMap.uitest in your project and validate that the control recorded is present.

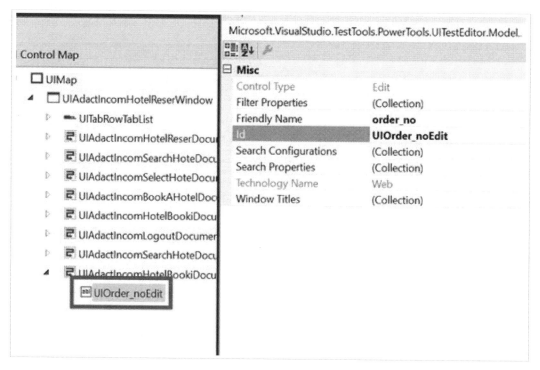

Figure 9.7 – View the recorded control

8. We can now use the control properties to get the booking number and add the booking number to the logs of the script. Add the below code to your script. Table 9.4 needs to be added to the beginning of the *Booking()* function where we are assigning local variables with the corresponding control elements present in the designer file.

```
HtmlEdit ul_OrderNo = this. UIAdactIncomBookAHotelWindow.
UIAdactIncomHotelBookiDocument.UIOrder_noEdit;
```

Table 9.3 – Add the code to get the Order number

9. Now that we have identified the booking order number, we will apply the concept of synchronization. After clicking the 'Book Now' button, our script should wait until the order number appears.

10. We will make use of method *WaitForControlExist()* and our new code will look like below -

```
// Click 'Book Now' button

Mouse.Click(uIBookNowButton, newPoint(76, 10));

//Playback.Wait(5000);

                 uI_OrderNo.SearchConfigurations.Add(SearchConfiguration.
AlwaysSearch);


if (uI_OrderNo.WaitForControlExist(10000))

        {

Mouse.Click(uILogoutHyperlink, newPoint(30, 13));


// Wait for 5 seconds for user delay between actions; Click 'Click here to login
again' link

Playback.Wait(5000);

Mouse.Click(uIClickheretologinagaiHyperlink, newPoint(190, 11));

        }
```

Table 9.4 – Using *WaitForControlExist method*

Note: Note that we have commented the following line –

//Playback.Wait(5000);

After commenting this line we have synchronized our code to wait for the order number textbox to exist before performing the next steps. We are using an If block to handle the code more appropriately in case there is an error and the control is not found.

if (uI_OrderNo.WaitForControlExist(10000))

Note:uI_OrderNo.SearchConfigurations.Add(SearchConfiguration. AlwaysSearch)is used to make sure that the UI test playback engine does not use a cached control to perform any search action.

11. Once we add this, we need to send the value of this text box to the console. Alternative ways of logging a message will be presented after this method.

```
if (ul_OrderNo.WaitForControlExist(10000))

    {

Console.WriteLine(ul_OrderNo.Text);

Mouse.Click(ulLogoutHyperlink, newPoint(30, 13));


// Wait for 5 seconds for user delay between actions; Click 'Click here to login again' link

Playback.Wait(5000);

Mouse.Click(ulClickheretologinagaiHyperlink, newPoint(190, 11));

    }

else

Console.WriteLine("Time out occured - Booking failed.");
```

Table 9.5 – Writing Order number to console

12. Let us execute our code and see the output in the 'Test Explorer' window. After successful execution, we should see something like this –

Figure 9.8 – View result

13. Observe the 'Output' link highlighted above. Click on this link. You will be taken to the Output window where you will see the booking order number–

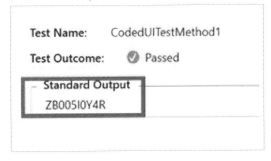

Test Name: CodedUITestMethod1

Test Outcome: ⊘ Passed

Standard Output

ZB005I0Y4R

Figure 9.9 – View Order number in output

Logging in Coded UI

It is necessary to understand how to log a message from a Coded UI Test for tracing\ debugging purposes. Here are five ways of doing this from any test type (Coded UI Test, Unit Test etc).

- **Console.WriteLine("My Message") / Console.Error.WriteLine("My Message")**

  Although these work, they are very tricky. The test harness redirects the Standard Output and Standard Error to capture the output\error from your product code and not for tracing. So, the recommendation is to avoid using these.

- **Trace.WriteLine("My Message")**

  This log shows up in the Visual Studio Output window during debugging. However, the message here could be lost among other trace messages from other components (or product codes). It is therefore recommended for use in your product code but not in your test code. This is a good way to separate product code messages from test code messages.

- **Debug.WriteLine("My Message")**

  This method is the same as *Trace.WriteLine* except that it shows up only for the Debug build.

- **TestContext.WriteLine("My Message")**

  This method displays the output/logs in the separate section in test result. It is intended this purpose only. To use this, you will have to pass a TestContext variable from your main test class to other classes. Visual Studio creates a reference of this variable by default in CodedUITest1.cs. This is the preferred method for tracing.

Exercise

1. Replace all the implicit wait commands with explicit waits.

❧

10.

Data Driven Framework

Introduction

In many instances, when we are performing regression testing, we need to repeat the same test case with different sets of data. This can be a monotonous and time-consuming task, depending on how many different data sets are required for the test case.

Example

Let us take an example:

We worked for one of our retail domain clients as part of the testing and automation team which had more than 2000 stores in the country. They had developed a point of sales system. Once this was manually tested, they gave us a list of more than 10000 usernames and password pairs, and asked us to set them up in the system. Our task was to verify if all usernames and passwords were set up correctly. We were given a.01% failure threshold target. If we had to verify all this manually, assuming we would verify 1 username/password combination every 1 minute (as there were a couple of validations we had to do once logged in), it would have taken us 5000 minutes or approximately 20-24 days of man effort. Imagine how laborious and time-consuming that task would have been.

Solution: Wouldn't it be great if you had an automated script to could pick up the first username and password entered from an excel sheet, log the user in and perform all the validations without any manual intervention?

An even better solution would be to create a script to iterate across all the 10000 usernames and passwords. It took us less than 4 hours to develop the script, ran it overnight, got the failed records, again re-tested the records once fixed and delivered it to the customer with 0% issues. The concept of running the same script with multiple dataset values is called **Parameterization**.

Any test case which needs to be executed multiple times with different data values is an ideal candidate for automation.

Another objective of Data Driven tests is to keep all of the test data in one central location.

Example

Let us take another example

Suppose you have 200+ scripts and all the scripts start with login which needs a username and password. Where should you keep this test data? If this data is residing within the script, and for some reason your username or password changes, then you would need to go into each script and make these changes.

Is there a better solution?

Wouldn't it be nice if you could have all of this data in one central file so that all of the scripts which need a username/password refer to just one file? If any of the usernames/passwords change, then we just make the change(s) at one location and all of the scripts will be good to go.

Key objectives:

- How to parameterize a Coded UI script to execute the same steps for multiple sets of data
- Writing custom functions

10.1 Adding a CSV file to your Coded UI Project

We will start by creating a new project under the solution 'MyFirstScript'. Let us follow the same procedure as in previous chapters. This time we will name the new project 'DataDrivenFramework'.

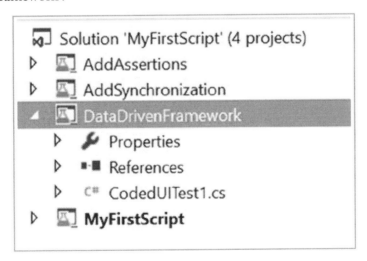

Figure 10.1 – Create a new project

Copy the UIMap.uitest file from the 'AddSynchronization' project created in the last chapter. Update the namespace references and CodedUITest1.cs file. The project should now compile successfully.

Let us now add a csv file into your new project. Visual Studio allows you to add an existing file to your project or add a new file to your project.

We will now add a new Text file to the project. Right-click on your project 'DataDrivenFramework' and select 'New Item'. This is depicted below –

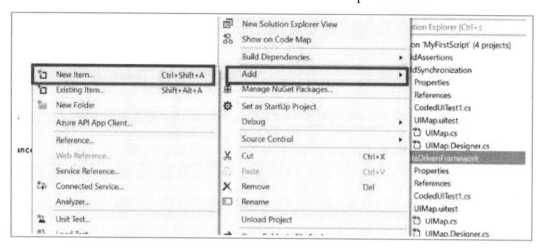

Figure 10.2 – Add a csv file to your project

The **Add New Item** dialog box opens up. In this dialog box select **General** on the left hand side. Then scroll down and select **Text File**. Now enter **Data File.csv** for the name of the file and click the **Add** button.

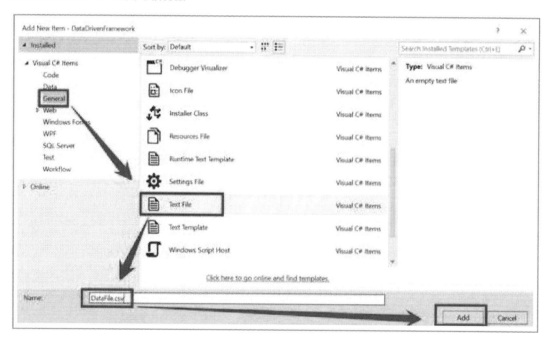

Figure 10.3 – Provide a name to your csv file

The DataFile.csv file stores data in the following format:

ID,Location

1,Sydney

2,Brisbane

3,Melbourne

4,Adelaide

Save the project. Right-click on **DataFile.csv** and select**Properties**.

Change Build Action to *Content* and Copy to Output Directory as *Copy if newer*. This is selected so the project identifies the data file as a content file and whenever the csv file is updated, it will be copied to the release/debug folder of the project.

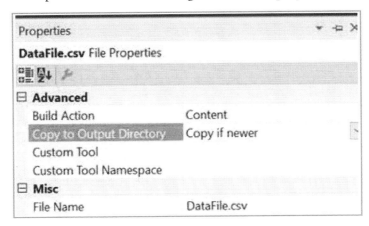

Figure 10.4 – Copy csv file to output directory

After we finish setting up the **DataFile.csv** file, we will update our code so that it recognizes the csv file. To do that we have to remove the [TestMethod] attribute above the CodedUITestMethod1() function and replace it with the following –

```
[DataSource("Microsoft.VisualStudio.TestTools.DataSource.CSV",
"|DataDirectory|\\DataFile.csv", "DataFile#csv", DataAccessMethod.
Sequential), DeploymentItem("DataFile.csv"), TestMethod]

public void CodedUITestMethod1()

    {

this.UIMap.Login();

this.UIMap.MyFirstAssert();

this.UIMap.Booking();
```

```
// To generate code for this test, select "Generate Code for Coded UI
Test" from the shortcut menu and select one of the menu items.

    }
```

Table 10.1 – Binding csy file with your project

We have binded our data source by using the *DataSource* attribute above.

The Coded UI test method will now recognize the DataFile.csv. To access the data in the csv file we can use the following code –

```
TestContext.DataRow["Location"].ToString();
```

The above code will return the first value of *Location* from the csv file.

Using DataFile.csv in your project

The datafile.csv file can now be used in the project by substituting the hard-coded value of 'Sydney' with values from the csv file. In this project we have selected 'Sydney' as the location and this appears in the UIMap.cs file. Open the UIMap.cs file and search for 'Sydney'. You will observe that this value is hard-coded –

```
public string UILocationComboBoxSelected Item = "Sydney";
```

If you now search for *UILocationComboBoxSelectedItem*, you will find that this combo box value is used by *uILocationComboBox* –

```
uILocationComboBox.SelectedItem = this.BookingParams.
UILocationComboBoxSelectedItem;
```

Now instead of feeding the hard-coded value to the location combo-box, let us use the values from the DataFile.csv file. To do that, we need to pass the *TestContext* parameter from *CodedUITest1.cs* to *UIMap.cs*. In *CodedUITest1.cs,* pass the parameter *TestContext* in the *Booking* function –

```
this.UIMap.Booking(TestContext);
```

Now, open the **UIMap.cs** file and create a *TestContext* parameter *tContext*in the *Booking* function –

```
public void Booking(TestContext tContext)
```

Now, we can use the variable *tContext* to read the content of the csv file. Our new code with parameterization should look like this –

```
uILocationComboBox.SelectedItem = tContext.DataRow["Location"].ToString();
```

Interesting thing here is that your project will execute all the rows of this csv file automatically.

Execute your script now. The script will take all 4 locations present in the csv file and will run sequentially.

Once executed, the Test Explorer window will show case all four runs for each data row as shown below –

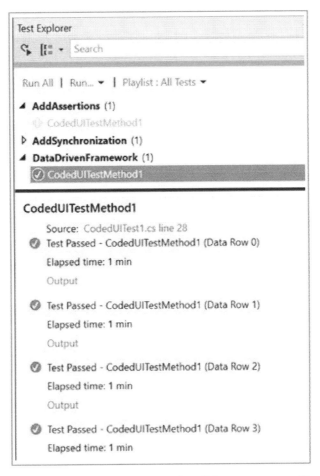

Figure 10.5 – Executing script for all locations in csv file

10.2 Writing helper functions in Coded UI Project

Functions help divide your test into logical units, such as areas of key functionalities of the application. Functions help make our scripts modular and reusable, which will save us maintenance effort and also help us improve productivity. These functions can then be re-used in different scripts.

For example, all of our scripts will have to login to the application. Now, instead of recording login steps repeatedly in every script, we can keep an external login function and re-use that function in all of our scripts. We have done the same in our script as shown below –

```
this.UIMap.Login();
```

In your project, you might need to add custom functions or helper functions.

Helper functions are used to reuse computations, just as with functions in general. These functions can perform numerous user-specific tasks.

Example

Let us see another practical example here. In the above section, we read the data from a csv file and pushed the value for *Location* in the **UIMap.cs** file. However, if we need to put a restriction on a particular value, then we need to write our own function for the same task.

To perform the same, let us add a new class to our project. This class can be named **Functions.cs.**

1. Right-click on your project and select **Add Class**.

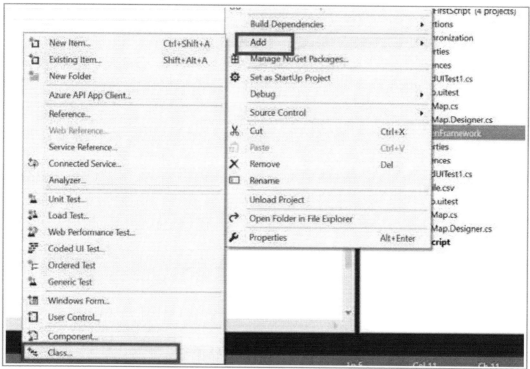

Figure 10.6 – Adding a new class to your project

2. Name the class **Functions.cs**. The class will be created.

3. We will now make this a static class as this will be reused multiple times in our project.

4. We will create a function **ReadDataFromCSV()**. This function will return *True* if the value of **Location** is *Sydney or* else will return *false*. The complete code is given below –

```
public static class Functions

    {
// Returns true when Sydney location is encountered in DataFile.csv

public static bool ReadDataFromCSV(TestContext tContext)

        {
bool bReturn = false;

try

            {
string strValue = tContext.DataRow["Location"].ToString();

if (String.Equals(strValue, "Sydney", StringComparison.OrdinalIgnoreCase))

                bReturn = true;

            }
catch (Exception e)

            {
Console.WriteLine("Error occured: " + e.Message);

                bReturn = true;

            }
return bReturn;

        }
    }
```

Table 10.2 – Adding custom function to Functions.cs

Note: In the class Functions.cs we have to add – using Microsoft. VisualStudio.TestTools.UnitTesting; at the top of the file. This way our function will recognize the TestContext class.

5. Observe, that the function ReadDataFromCSV() can now be used anywhere in your project. E.g. if your code needs to execute only when the location is 'Sydney', then we can add this code in **CodedUITest1.cs** –

```
public void CodedUITestMethod1()

    {

if (Functions.ReadDataFromCSV(TestContext))

        {

this.UIMap.Login();

this.UIMap.MyFirstAssert();

this.UIMap.Booking(TestContext);

        }

// To generate code for this test, select "Generate Code for Coded UI Test" from the
shortcut menu and select one of the menu items.

    }
```

Table 10.3 – Using custom function from Functions.cs

We have added an *if* condition in the above code. This will skip all the location values except 'Sydney' and the test case will pass.

Exercise

1. Use the DataFile.csv file to store hotel names as well as the locations. Read the hotel name from the csv file in your Coded UI script.

෴

11.

Handling Pop-up Dialogs and Image Capture

Most of the modern day applications come with various pop-up messages and multiple windows.

For instance, if you would like to delete a record in your application many applications will throw a javascript based confirmation pop-up dialog before deletion.

Also applications these days have child pop-up windows.

Example

We were once automating a mortgage based Web application, which had search customer functionality. When a user clicks on the search link it opens a new pop-up window in which the user could search and select any customer. After the customer was selected the pop-up window would close and the user would return to the main Web page.

How would Coded UI work in these scenarios?

Second part of this chapter will illustrate how to capture screenshot.

Example

We had a client who wanted us to do take screenshots of all the critical Web pages on different browsers (Chrome, Firefox and IE) and store them at a central location which could be analyzed by a business analyst. So the question was whether Coded UI can assist us in taking snapshots.

In this chapter we will see

- How Coded UI works with Alert dialogs
- How Coded UI captures images

11.1 Handling Alerts or Prompts

Test Scenario – Follow the steps below in the Hotel Application

- Login

- Search for the hotel
- Select Hotel
- In the Booking form enter required details but enter Credit Card expiry year as 2011
- Click on Book Now. You will see a pop-up window

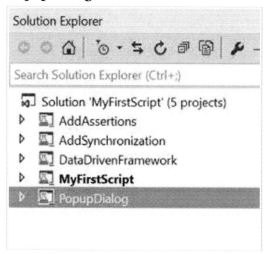

Figure 11-1 – Pop-up dialog

- While the pop-up dialog is open, try to click the Logout link or any other link. You will notice that all other links are disabled since the focus is on the pop-up dialog

Now we will see how to handle this pop-up dialog using Coded UI.

1. We will start by creating a new project under the solution 'MyFirstScript'.

2. Let us follow the same procedure as in previous chapters. This time we will name the new project **'PopupDialog'**.

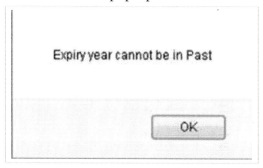

Figure **11.2** – Create a new project

3. Copy UIMap.uitest from the 'AddSynchronization' project created in the last chapter.

4. Update the namespace references and CodedUITest1.cs file.

5. The project should now compile successfully.

6. In this 'PopupDialog' project, open the UIMap.cs file. This file contains an entry '2018' which is used for the credit card's expiry year –

```
public string UICc_exp_yearComboBoxSelectedItem = "2018";
```

Table 11.1 – Editing expiry year of credit card

7. Modify the CreditCard Expiry Year from "2018" to "2011" to simulate the scenario.

8. When you execute the script now, the output will be a successful run with a message in the output window saying – '**Time out occured - Booking failed.**'

9. The script is successful because we have added logic to the script to write a log entry if the booking is unsuccessful.

Let us see how we can handle pop-up dialogs.

Coded UI Test Builder

1. This is a standard Record and Play method in which we can record the pop-up dialogs and use them in our code in whatever way we want. Find below the screenshot that depicts the way to capture the pop-up dialog into our script –

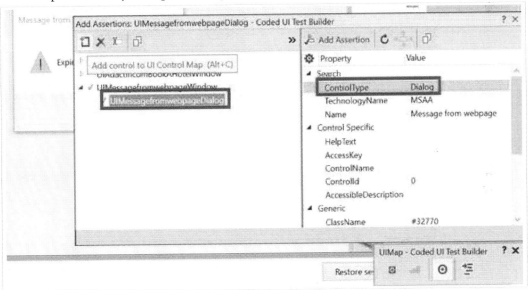

Figure 11.3 – Recording pop-up dialog using Coded UI Test Builder

We will not be recording a pop-up dialog here and are leaving it for you to do. We will however look at the generic ways of identifying and handling the pop-up dialogs in our scripts.

BrowserWindow

2. When the 'Book Now' button is clicked in our script, the booking is successful or unsuccessful or we get a warning **pop-up dialog** box. Let us make our script identify all three scenarios. For this, we need to understand the below mentioned code –

```
BrowserWindow browserWindow = new BrowserWindow();

browserWindow.PerformDialogAction(BrowserDialogAction.Ok);
```

Table 11.2 – Using PerformDialogAction method

In this code, we are creating an object of type **BrowserWindow**. If our website opens a pop-up dialog box, the *browserWindow* object will click the OK button in the pop-up dialog box. Otherwise our code will continue working on the next steps (see PlaybackSettings in the next section). This code can be used to handle un-expected pop-up dialogs in your script. They can additionally be used to capture warning/error messages in an AUT.

PlaybackSettings

3. Before moving further, we should also understand the concept of PlaybackSettings in Coded UI. There are various settings for Playback and we can modify them to improve the resilience of Coded UI Tests. Playback is configured by modifying the fields in the **Playback.PlaybackSettings** class. Various properties of this class are defined below –

Name	Description
ContinueOnError	Gets or sets a flag which indicates whether to ignore playback related failures that occur during a playback session.
DelayBetweenActions	Gets or sets the delay between actions in milliseconds.
ImeLanguageList	Gets a list of Input Method Editors(IME) language locale IDs(LCID) for which IME ends composition on clicking the {Enter} key.
LoggerOverrideState	This State will maintain overrides to HtmlLoggerState. Will get preference over Eqt Trace when overridden.
MatchExactHierarchy	Gets or sets a value to indicate whether to match the exact hierarchy specified for searching this control.

MaximumRetryCount	Gets or sets the number of times a retry can be done for a single action via PlaybackError handler in a Coded UI test.
SearchInMinimizedWindows	Gets or sets a value that indicates whether to search in minimized windows.
SearchTimeout	Gets or sets the time-out for searches.
SendKeysAsScanCode	Gets or sets a value indicating whether to send the keys as a scan-code.
ShouldSearchFailFast	Gets or sets a value indicating whether search has to fail fast or after the timeout period set for the search operation has elapsed.
SkipSetPropertyVerification	Gets or sets a value indicating whether to skip verification after a set value.
SmartMatchOptions	Gets or sets a value that indicates whether smart match is enabled.
ThinkTimeMultiplier	Gets or sets the think time multiplier.
WaitForReadyLevel	Gets or sets the *WaitForReadyLevel* to be used for *WaitForReady* calls during a search operation.
WaitForReadyTimeout	Gets or sets the number of milliseconds to wait for the application to be ready.

Table 11.3 – Properties of PlaybackSettings class

Note: More details on these methods can be found at the link - https://msdn.microsoft.com/en-us/library/microsoft.visualstudio. testtools.uitesting.playbacksettings.aspx

4. We will use the **ContinueOnError** property of the PlaybackSettings class in our script.

5. We will change our code so that it handles the pop-up dialog box (if encountered) while logging the corresponding activity. Find below the updated code.

```
// Click 'Book Now' button

Mouse.Click(uIBookNowButton, newPoint(76, 10));

//Playback.Wait(5000);

        ul_OrderNo.SearchConfigurations.Add(SearchConfiguration.AlwaysSearch);


try

        {

BrowserWindow browserWindow = newBrowserWindow();

                browserWindow.PerformDialogAction(BrowserDialogAction.Ok);

Console.WriteLine("Popup dialog appeared.");

        }

catch (Exception)

        {

Console.WriteLine("Popup dialog did not appear.");

Playback.PlaybackSettings.ContinueOnError = true;

        }



if (ul_OrderNo.WaitForControlExist(10000))

        {

Console.WriteLine("Booking Successful - " + ul_OrderNo.Text);

        }

else

        {

Console.WriteLine("Time out occurred - Booking failed.");

        }

Mouse.Click(uILogoutHyperlink, newPoint(30, 13));
```

> // Wait for 5 seconds for user delay between actions; Click 'Click here to login again' link
>
> Playback.Wait(5000);
>
> Mouse.Click(uIClickheretologinagaiHyperlink, newPoint(190, 11));

Table 11.4 – Applying ContinueOnError method

6. This code handles all the pop-up dialog scenarios and writes the correct message to the output for each scenario. The output for a failed booking will look like this –

Test Name: CodedUITestMethod1

Test Outcome: ✅ Passed

Standard Output

Popup dialog appeared.
Time out occured - Booking failed.

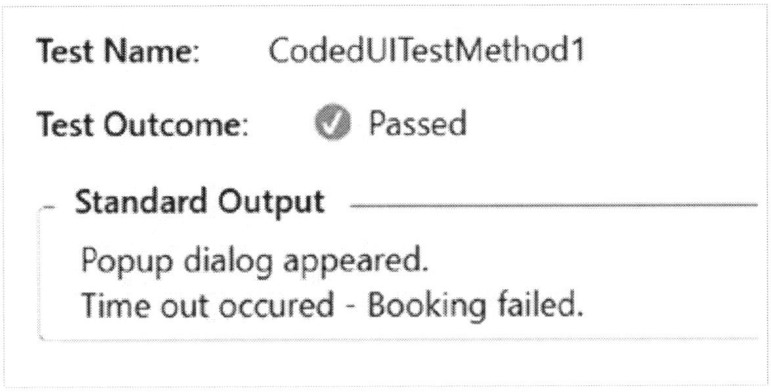

Figure 11.4 – Result of a failed booking

7. The output for a successful booking will look like this –

Test Name: CodedUITestMethod1

Test Outcome: ✅ Passed

Standard Output

Popup dialog did not appeared.
Booking Successful - 16ZMJ32TFV

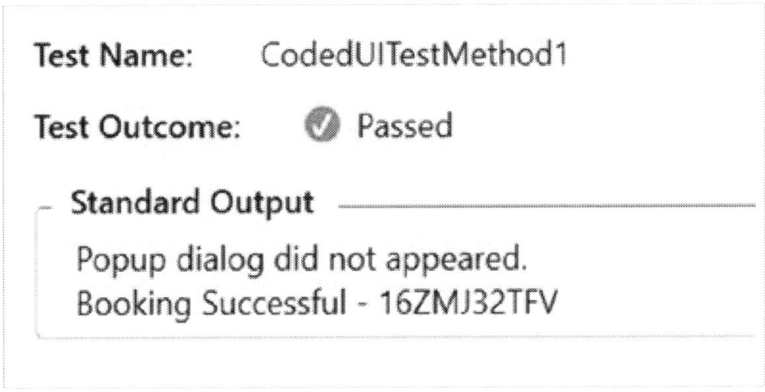

Figure 11.5 – Result of a successful booking

11.2 Capturing Images in Coded UI

This section will describe how to capture a screenshot of the window or UI control when the script is running. To accomplish this we will use the CaptureImage() method provided by Visual Studio.

Let us take an example from the previous section. When our script clicks the **Book Now** button and a pop-up dialog box opens, it would be natural for the user to analyse the pop-up dialog box. This could be done with the help of a screenshot.

CaptureImage() method

The **UIControl.CaptureImage()** method returns an object of the type Image. This object needs to be saved at a location to access it. The user can optionally provide the image format as well.

The updated code of our script should look like this –

```
Try

    {


BrowserWindow browserWindow = newBrowserWindow();

Image imgScreenshot = browserWindow.CaptureImage();

        imgScreenshot.Save("C:/scripts/popupdialog.jpg");

        browserWindow.PerformDialogAction(BrowserDialogAction.Ok);

Console.WriteLine("Popup dialog appeared.");

    }

catch (Exception)

    {

Console.WriteLine("Popup dialog did not appear.");

Playback.PlaybackSettings.ContinueOnError = true;

    }



if (uI_OrderNo.WaitForControlExist(10000))

    {

Console.WriteLine("Booking Successful - " + uI_OrderNo.Text);

Image imgScreenshot = uI_OrderNo.CaptureImage();

        imgScreenshot.Save("C:/scripts/bookingdetails.jpg");
```

```
        }
else

        {
Console.WriteLine("Time out occurred - Booking failed.");

        }
Mouse.Click(uiLogoutHyperlink, newPoint(30, 13));


// Wait for 5 seconds for user delay between actions; Click 'Click here to login
again' link
Playback.Wait(5000);
Mouse.Click(uiClickheretologinagaiHyperlink, newPoint(190, 11));
```

Table **11.5** – Capture and Save method for screenshot

In the code above, we will capture the pop-up dialog box if it appears. We will also capture the text box that displays the booking number when the booking is successful. The screenshots will be saved to the **"C:\Scripts\"** folder on your system. We can use the methods to intuitively modify our code and create generic methods to capture screenshots.

When the booking is successful, we will have the following screenshot (*bookingdetails.jpg*) –

Figure **11.6** – Screenshot of Order number UI Control

Capturing pop-up dialog

The pop-up dialog screenshot will be captured each time. The reason for this is our code does not distinguish between an actual pop-up dialog box and the current browser window. Therefore *popupdialog.jpg* is just a screen capture each time the script executes. We can, however, customize our code as per the business requirements. The screenshot would look like this –

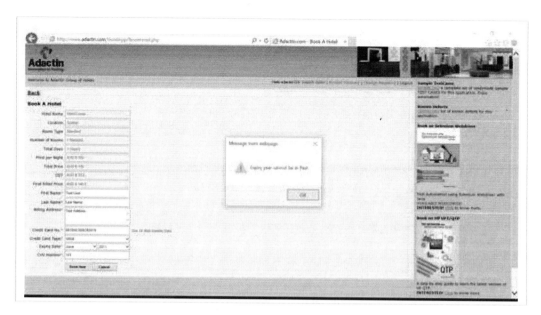

Figure 11.7 – Screenshot of Pop-up dialog

In this chapter we looked at ways to handle pop-up dialogs/message boxes. We also looked at ways to capture screenshots. We should now be able to implement both of these actions in our projects.

Exercise

1. Use Image Capture with all the assertion points in your script.

ço

12.

Working with User Interface Controls

Introduction

We know how Coded UI works as a tool, and recognizes Web elements based on properties and its values. In a Coded UI script, the Web element property values are located within the script. For instance, when we login, the *username* web element's property gets added locally within the script statement. We can view the same on UIMap.uitest as shown below-

> Type 'adactin123' in username textbox

In the above statement, the property values for *username* are located within the script. UI Map is used to store object properties.

What if due to business requirements, the developer changes the property value of these Web elements? For instance, add a new web element called 'customername'. This would result in a requirement to record this element in order to use it.

A better solution would be if we keep all the required Web elements and their properties in an external location/file and all the scripts could just use Web element properties from this shared location. This will certainly avoid redundancy. Also, if any Web element changes, we would only need to change the Web element once and the script will be working again.

Example

For one of our clients for whom we had to implement automation, we were given 100 existing automation scripts. We were told that the scripts used to work 3 months earlier, but now, they fail on new builds. We were asked to fix the scripts. Guess what we found? All the scripts were using local Web element properties. When we identified the Web elements that were causing the script to fail, we discovered that the same Web element was used in all 100 scripts. So the Web element had to be modified at least 100 times as it was being used in all the scripts. But there were at least 100 Web elements, which had changed. Adding to this, they informed us that UI (user interface) changes were still happening and that the Web elements will change again. Our recommendation to them was to hold on and to re-do the scripts using a hand coded UI Map. The advice stemmed from the fact that the same effort invested now would be required again when we get a new application build, with updated Web elements. Yes, it did mean that most of the previous efforts already made had been wasted. But our re-scripting approach, using a custom created Web Element Map, ensured that script maintenance was future proofed.

In this chapter we will see how to Add a web control to Coded UI script

12.1 Add a web control to Coded UI script

We will start by creating a new project under the solution 'MyFirstScript'. Let us follow the same procedure as in previous chapters. This time we will name the new project 'AddWebControl'.

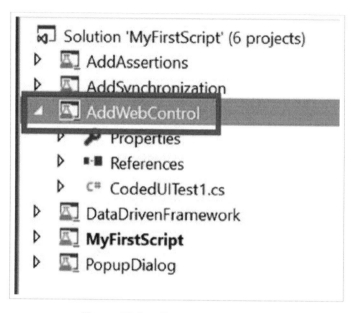

Figure 12.1 – Create a new project

Copy the UIMap.uitest file from the 'AddSynchronization' project created in the last chapter. Update the namespace references and CodedUITest1.cs file. The project should now compile successfully.

We will now use the already recorded script in this project. In addition, we will include the click on **Reset** button. Our script should have the following steps –

   a. Login (Use the username/password that you registered earlier).

   b. Search for Hotel.

       i. Select a location, e.g., Sydney

      ii. Select number of rooms, e.g., 2-Two

     iii. Select adults per rooms, e.g., 2-Two

     iv. Click the Search button

   c. Click the **Reset** button.

   d. Search for Hotel.

       i. Select a location, e.g., Sydney

    ii.   Select number of rooms, e.g., 2-Two

    iii. Select adults per rooms, e.g., 2-Two

    iv. Click the Search button

e. Select a Hotel.

    i.   Select one of the Hotel Radio buttons, e.g., select radio button next to Hotel Creek.

f. Book a Hotel.

    i.   Enter First Name

    ii.   Enter Last Name

    iii. Enter Address

    iv. Enter 16-digit Credit Card no:

    v.   Enter Credit Card type

    vi. Enter Expiry Month

    vii. Enter Expiry Year

    viii.Enter CVV number

    ix. Click on Book Now

g. After you see the Booking confirmation page, click theLogout link in the top right corner

h. Click the"Click here to Login again" link to go back to the Home page.

In this script, we are using our old workflow, except in points **c & d**.

In this section, we will manually identify and add the properties for the Reset button and then use them in our script. This will be a three step process –

1. Identify HTML properties of the Reset button.

2. Create a UI element in UIMap.cs so that Coded UI is able to identify the Reset button.

3. Modify the existing script to accommodate clicking the Reset button.

Identify HTML properties of the Reset button

To identify the properties of the **Reset** button,

- Login to the Hotel App.
- Go to the Search Hotel page.
- Right-click the Reset button.
- Select Inspect element.

Figure **12.2** – Inspect properties of Reset button

- Observe the HTML properties of the Reset button.

```
<input name="Reset" class="reg_button" id="Reset" type="reset" value="Reset" />
```

Figure 12.3 – Properties of Reset button in web browser

Create a UI element in UIMap.cs

Once we have identified the properties of the Reset button, we will hand code an element in the **UIMap.cs** file. We will create a new instance of **UITestControl**. UITestControl class provides the ability to locate controls on a User Interface. To enable your Coded UI script to identify a new element, we need to perform the following steps –

- Instantiate an object of type UITestControl.
- Provide the container (Browser Window).
- Add Search properties.
- Perform *click* operation.

Here is the sample code for the above steps –

```
UITestControl uiButtonReset = new UITestControl(browserWindow);

uiButtonReset.TechnologyName = "Web";

uiButtonReset.SearchProperties.Add("Id","Reset");

uiButtonReset.SearchProperties.Add("Name", "Reset");

uiButtonReset.SearchProperties.Add("Class", "reg_button");

Mouse.Click(uiButtonReset);
```

Table 12.1 – Adding UI control to Coded UI script

In the above code, we have added the values for Id, Name and Class from the HTML properties identified previously.

> **Note**: Note the *browserWindow* object we have passed in UITestControl. This is a container window where my script is running. We have to modify our existing script to accommodate the *browserWindow* object. We will discuss this in the next section.

Modify existing script

Now we have identified HTML properties of a new web element and understand the corresponding code required to be added in Coded UI. Before moving forward, we need to help our code understand the container or browser window where our script is being executed (in this case Internet Explorer).

Search for this code in **UIMap.cs** -

```
// Go to web page 'http://www.adactin.com/HotelApp/index.php' using new browser instance

this.UIAdactIncomBookAHotelWindow.LaunchUrl(new      System.Uri(this.
LoginParams.UIAdactIncomBookAHotelWindowUrl));
```

Table 12.2 – View the browser window object in our Coded UI script

In the code above, the Coded UI script is initiating a new browser window with the Hotel App URL. We will modify the code to do the same thing but will get the browser window as a return variable.

The modified code is shown below with the changes marked in bold –

```
private BookingParams mBookingParams;

private BrowserWindow browserWindow;


///<summary>

/// Login - Use 'LoginParams' to pass parameters into this method.

///</summary>

public void Login()

        {

#region Variable Declarations

HtmlEdit uIUsernameEdit = this.UIAdactIncomBookAHotelWindow.
UIAdactIncomHotelReserDocument.UIUsernameEdit;

HtmlEdit uIPasswordEdit = this.UIAdactIncomBookAHotelWindow.
UIAdactIncomHotelReserDocument.UIPasswordEdit;

HtmlInputButton uILoginButton = this.UIAdactIncomBookAHotelWindow.
UIAdactIncomHotelReserDocument.UILoginButton;

#endregion


// Go to web page 'http://www.adactin.com/HotelApp/index.php' using new
browser instance

browserWindow = BrowserWindow.Launch(new System.Uri(this.
LoginParams.UIAdactIncomBookAHotelWindowUrl));

//this.UIAdactIncomBookAHotelWindow.LaunchUrl(new System.Uri(this.
LoginParams.UIAdactIncomBookAHotelWindowUrl));
```

Table 12.3 – Add code to launch Browser Window

With the above changes (in Bold), we have an object **browserWindow** that contains the browser window object that is under test. We will use this object to instantiate the **UITestControl** object.

We will now go to the location in the UIMap.cs file where we are entering the 'Search Hotel' criteria. Find the following location in your code –

```
// Wait for 5 seconds for user delay between actions; Select 'Sydney' in
'location' combo box

Playback.Wait(5000);

ulLocationComboBox.SelectedItem = this.BookingParams.
UILocationComboBoxSelectedItem;


// Select '2 - Two' in 'adult_room' combo box

ulAdult_roomComboBox.SelectedItem = this.BookingParams.UIAdult_
roomComboBoxSelectedItem;


// Select '2 - Two' in 'child_room' combo box

ulChild_roomComboBox.SelectedItem = this.BookingParams.UIChild_
roomComboBoxSelectedItem;
```

Table 12.4 – Locate Search hotel code in script

The idea now is to enter the search criteria, click on the rest button and enter the search criteria again. Find below the modified code to achieve the same –

```
// Wait for 5 seconds for user delay between actions; Select 'Sydney' in
'location' combo box

Playback.Wait(5000);

ulLocationComboBox.SelectedItem = this.BookingParams.
UILocationComboBoxSelectedItem;


// Select '2 - Two' in 'adult_room' combo box

ulAdult_roomComboBox.SelectedItem = this.BookingParams.UIAdult_
roomComboBoxSelectedItem;


// Select '2 - Two' in 'child_room' combo box

ulChild_roomComboBox.SelectedItem = this.BookingParams.UIChild_
roomComboBoxSelectedItem;
```

```
UITestControl uiButtonReset = new UITestControl(browserWindow);

uiButtonReset.TechnologyName = "Web";

uiButtonReset.SearchProperties.Add("Id","Reset");

uiButtonReset.SearchProperties.Add("Name", "Reset");

uiButtonReset.SearchProperties.Add("Class", "reg_button");

Mouse.Click(uiButtonReset);


// Wait for 5 seconds for user delay between actions; Select 'Sydney' in
'location' combo box

Playback.Wait(5000);

uILocationComboBox.SelectedItem = this.BookingParams.
UILocationComboBoxSelectedItem;


// Select '2 - Two' in 'adult_room' combo box

uiAdult_roomComboBox.SelectedItem = this.BookingParams.UIAdult_
roomComboBoxSelectedItem;


// Select '2 - Two' in 'child_room' combo box

uIChild_roomComboBox.SelectedItem = this.BookingParams.UIChild_
roomComboBoxSelectedItem;


// Click 'Search' button

Mouse.Click(uISearchButton, newPoint(46, 11));
```

Table 12.5 – Add code for Reset button in Coded UI script

Observe the code marked in **bold** above. This code will search for the Reset button on the webpage and click it. We can go ahead and identify more controls and add them to our script. As a good design standard, we can create a separate class where object properties are defined.

Note: In this example, we used **Inspect element** of Internet Explorer to identify the HTML properties of a web element. We can also use the ⊚ button on **Coded UI Test Builder** widget to identify the properties of web elements.

Exercise

1. Create a new project. Implement Forgot Password script by utilizing Add web control functionality.

Multiple Choice Questions Set-2

1. Which method is used to insert an Assert in Coded UI Test Builder?

   A. Add Assert

   B. Add Assertion

   C. Assert Now

   D. Assert This

2. Select all the Comparators available in the Assertion dialog in Coded UI

   A. AreEqual

   B. AreSame

   C. Fail

   D. AreFail

3. Which is the StringAssert method used for comparing string values?

   A. Contains

   B. IsEqual

   C. Equals

   D. IsContain

4. Which method is used to insert an implicit delay during playback?

   A. WaitFor()

   B. Playback.Wait()

   C. Delay()

   D. Play.Wait()

5. Which of the statements is used for an explicit wait?

   A. WaitForControlReady

   B. Wait

   C. IsControlAvaialable

   D. All of the above

6. Which method writes a log to the output in Coded UI?

   A. WriteLog()

   B. Console.WriteLine()

   C. Log.Write()

   D. Write()

7. Which object property control type is used to handle a confirmation pop-up?

   A. Pop-up

   B. AlertWindow

   C. Dialog

   D. Childwindow

8. Which C# method is used to fetch the value for 'Location' from the csv file?

   A. DataRow["Location"]

   B. DataRow("Location")

   C. DataRow{"Location"}

   D. None of the above

9. How do we find HTML properties of a web element in Internet Explorer?

   A. Using Get Element

   B. Using Find Element

   C. Using Inspect Element

   D. Cannot find from browser

10. Which method is used by Coded UI to perform an operation on a pop-up dialog?

   A. browserWindow.DialogAction

   B. browserWindow.DoDialogAction

   C. browserWindow. Action

   D. browserWindow.PerformDialogAction

Answers

Q1. Answer: B

Explanation – Add Assertion method is provided in Coded UI Test Builder

Q2. Answer: A,B,C

Explanation – Multiple Comparator options are provided by Coded UI Test Builder

Q3. Answer: A

Explanation – Contains is a method provided by the StringAssert class

Q4. Answer: B

Explanation – Playback.Wait() is used to add an implicit wait between playback of recorded steps

Q5. Answer: A

Explanation – WaitForControlReady is one of the multiple explicit wait commands provided by Coded UI. This waits for control to be ready on the page

Q6. Answer: B

Explanation – Console.WriteLine() is a standard C# method to write a log to the console window

Q7. Answer: C

Explanation – When recording a pop-up dialog, Coded UI recognizes it as a Dialog type object

Q8. Answer: A

Explanation – In C# we use DataRow["Location"] to fetch values from a data table

Q9. Answer: C

Explanation – Right-click on the element in Internet Explorer and select option 'Inspect element'. This will open up the HTML and show the properties of the selected web element

Q10. Answer: D

Explanation – PerformDialogAction is a method exposed by C#'s BrowserWindow class. This is used to perform an operation on the pop-up dialog like clicking the OK or Cancel button

❦

13.

Debugging Scripts

Introduction

We believe one cannot be an expert in any tool if he or she does not know how to debug issues, or does not know how to troubleshoot problems encountered while using the tool.

Debugging is an integrated feature of any automation tool. Automation scripts do fail, and we should be able to pinpoint exactly where the issue is, so that it can be fixed.

Coded UI, within the Visual Studio Environment, comes with some clever debugging features, which should be used while isolating the reason a script failed. We would want to have the ability to execute one step at a time, pause at a particular step, or be able to peek at values of variables at runtime. All these features can be found within Visual Studio IDE.

Example

At one of our telecom clients, they had around 150 automation scripts, and they were not executable after a new build was released to the test team. The core automation team had left after the release and nobody knew how to fix the scripts. The only way we could figure out what went wrong with the script - and understand the application workflow - was by using the debugging features. This proved invaluable to us in getting the scripts up and running again!

In this chapter we will learn how to debug Coded UI scripts.

Key objectives:

- Debugging features
- Execute tests in debug mode
- Step commands, Variables and Watches

13.1 Debugging Features

Debugging allows you to run a program interactively while watching the source code and the variables during the execution. Basically, debugging is a way to pause the execution of a program so that we can examine its internals at that point in time to deduce what is going wrong. To that end, we have a few basic notions:

Breakpoints: These are locations in the code that we can specify where code execution will pause and we can examine the execution environment and gain manual control over the execution process. Setting a breakpoint in Visual Studio is as simple as right-clicking on the desired line of code and selecting Insert Breakpoint. We will see how to insert a Breakpoint in the next section. In support of breakpoints are two main control buttons:

- **Run**-- execute the code as normal until the next breakpoint is encountered
- **Stop**-- terminate the program execution completely

Execution Stepping: This manual control over the execution process allows us to advance the execution one line of code at a time. Visual Studio provides convenient buttons for stepping control. There are 3 ways of stepping that one uses most often:

- **Step Into**-- Advance to the next line of code, following the execution path into every method that is executed
- **Step Over**-- Advance to the next line of code, but do not go into any methods that are encountered
- **Step Out**-- Advance to the next line of code following the end of the current method in the calling method, i.e., finish the current method

Variables Inspection: Once execution has stopped by a breakpoint, we can examine all the variables, fields, and objects that are in scope (visible) at that moment. Visual Studio has a very nice "WatchWindow" for this job.

Expressions Inspection – Apart from variables you may also want to see the results of expressions. For example - the Variables tab will show you the value of variables 'a' and 'b', but if you want to evaluate and view the value of expression "a+b", we can see this using Visual Studio. Expressions are also referenced using the term "Watch" in programming tools.

Basic Debugging Procedure

There is no "one right way" to debug. Debugging is as much an art as it is a skill. One has to think like a detective, looking for clues and applying deductive reasoning to explain what you've found. Always remember that the location at which bugs manifest themselves as some sort of visible effect, is often not where the problem actually occurs. You must always keep an understanding of how all the pieces in your system relate to each other.

Most debugging scenarios can be broken down into these steps:

1. Set breakpoints at key locations in your code. Typical places to put breakpoints include:

   - Wherever the problem clearly manifests itself. If possible, put the breakpoint a few lines before the problematic line so you can step up to it in a controlled manner.

- Wherever the key objects are constructed or key relationships are being established. For instance, null pointer errors are always due to calling a method on an object reference that is null, i.e., it was never assigned or instantiated properly.

2. Examine all variables that are visible at the breakpoint location and make sure that their values are what you expect them to be.

3. Step slowly through your code, checking all your variables as you go. Watch for the unexpected! Remember, if your code did what you expected, it would have run without any errors.

4. Use Step Over and Step Return(Step Out Of) only when you are positive, i.e., you did a Step Into at least once and everything that is being skipped works properly. It is very common to get overconfident and miss where an error occurs because one has skipped right over the critical code.

5. Add more breakpoints when you see something amiss and you deduce that an error might be due to potential problems in another section of the code. You can use the "Continue" button to quickly advance to the next breakpoint.

By using breakpoints in the source code, you specify where the execution of the program should pause.Breakpoints and watchpoints can be summarized as pause points. Once the program is paused you can investigate variables, change their content, etc.

13.2 Run Tests in Debug mode with Breakpoints

In this section we will execute one of our scripts in Debug mode with Breakpoints.

1. **Create** a new project named **DebugModeCodedUI** under the solution MyFirstScript.

2. Copy **UIMap.uitest** from the AddWebControl project and paste into the **DebugModeCodedUI**project.

3. Update CodedUITest1.cs file in the **DebugModeCodedUI**project (see previous chapters).

4. Update namespace references in the **DebugModeCodedUI**project.

5. **Rebuild** the solution.

Breakpoints

6. Open **UIMap.cs** file. At the step where the user selects location ("Sydney") insert a breakpoint. To insert a breakpoint

   a. Single click on the leftmost vertical bar next to the line of code at which you want to insert the Breakpoint

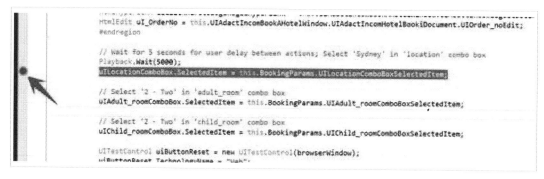

Figure 13.1 – Adding a breakpoint

b. Alternatively, select the step at which you would want to insert the Breakpoint, then select **Debug→Toggle Breakpoint.** The shortcut for this is to press **F9**.

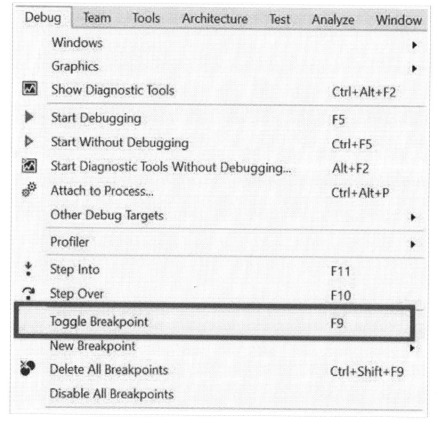

Figure 13.2 – Toolbar option to insert breakpoint

Debug Mode Run

6. Once the Breakpoint is inserted, let us execute the script in Debug mode. Open CodedUITest1.cs. Place your cursor inside **CodedUITestMethod1** method, right-click and Select **Debug Tests.**

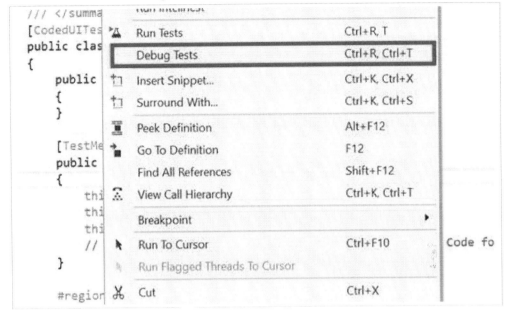

Figure 13.3 – Debugging scripts

Note: If we run the script in normal Run mode (**Run Tests**) our script would not pause at the breakpoint. It is only when we run our script in Debug mode that the script will pause at the breakpoint.

7. When the breakpoint is encountered, you will notice Visual Studio switches to debug perspective as in the snapshot below.

```
// Wait for 5 seconds for user delay between actions; Select 'Sydney' in 'location' combo box
Playback.Wait(5000);
uILocationComboBox.SelectedItem = this.BookingParams.UILocationComboBoxSelectedItem;

// Select '2 - Two' in 'adult_room' combo box
uIAdult_roomComboBox.SelectedItem = this.BookingParams.UIAdult_roomComboBoxSelectedItem;

// Select '2 - Two' in 'child_room' combo box
uIChild_roomComboBox.SelectedItem = this.BookingParams.UIChild_roomComboBoxSelectedItem;
```

Figure 13.4 – Breakpoint encountered during script execution

8. Go to your sample application and you will notice that execution is halted and the application is on the Search Hotel Page after logging in

9. Click on the **Continue** icon at the top left of the window

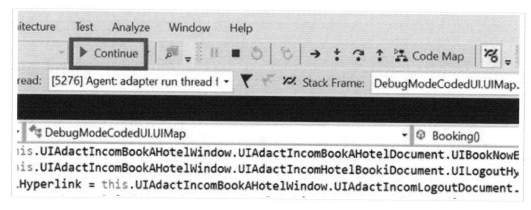

Figure 13.5 – Continue execution of a script

10. You will notice that the test runs until completion

> **Note:** Breakpoint insertion is useful when you are not sure of the state of your application at a particular step of your test run. After the script pauses at the breakpoint, the user can either choose to run the script until completion or run one step at a time.

13.3 Step Commands, Variables and Watch

Another benefit of running a script in debug mode is that the user can run a single step at a time which helps him to debug a specific part of the code which is causing the issue. We can achieve this using Step Into, Step Over, and Step Out commands.

Also, we can see the values stored in variables or values evaluated for expressions while running each step of our script. We can use the Watch window for this.

In the following steps we will see how to use Step commands and also how to see variable values.

1. Double-click on **UIMap.cs** to see the script.

2. Verify that there is a breakpoint at the step where the user selects a location ("Sydney"). If not, then insert a breakpoint as mentioned in the previous section.

3. Once the Breakpoint is inserted, let us execute the script in Debug mode. Open CodedUITest1.cs. Place your cursor inside **CodedUITestMethod1** method, right-click and Select **Debug Tests.**

4. Once the test starts running you will notice that the script will pause before executing the Breakpoint step.

5. You will notice Visual Studio switches to debug perspective. Now let's run one step at a time using Step Into, Step Over and Step Out option. We can see the same in **Debug** menu.

	Step Into	F11
	Step Over	F10
	Step Out	Shift+F11

Figure 13.6 – Debugging options in Visual Studio

Step Into (F11) -- Advance to the next line of code, following the execution path into every method that is executed

Step Over (F10) -- Advance to the next line of code, but do not go into any methods that are encountered

Step Out (Shift+F11) -- Advance to the next line of code following the end of the current method in the calling method, i.e., finish the current method

6. Let us use the Step Over (F10) command to run over each step without getting into any underlying methods. Click the **Step Over** iconor press **F10.**

7. You will notice that the script has moved on to the next step and has again paused waiting for user action.

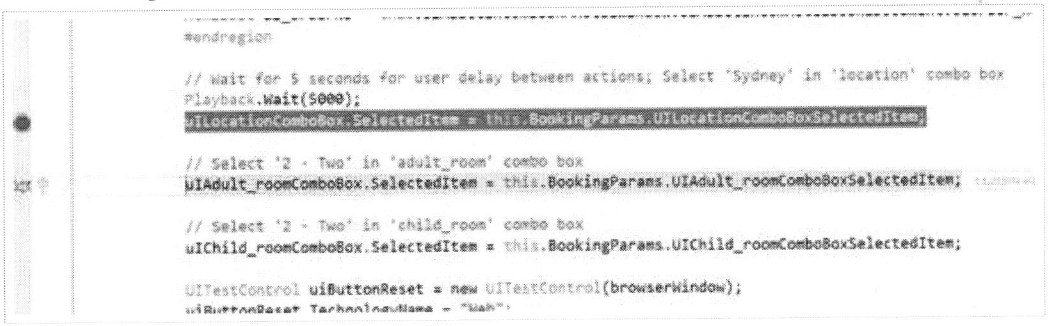

```
#endregion

// Wait for 5 seconds for user delay between actions; Select 'Sydney' in 'location' combo box
Playback.Wait(5000);
uILocationComboBox.SelectedItem = this.BookingParams.UILocationComboBoxSelectedItem;

// Select '2 - Two' in 'adult_room' combo box
uIAdult_roomComboBox.SelectedItem = this.BookingParams.UIAdult_roomComboBoxSelectedItem;

// Select '2 - Two' in 'child_room' combo box
uIChild_roomComboBox.SelectedItem = this.BookingParams.UIChild_roomComboBoxSelectedItem;

UITestControl uiButtonReset = new UITestControl(browserWindow);
uiButtonReset.TechnologyName = "Web";
```

Figure 13.7 – Debugging multiple breakpoints

8. You can continue to press **F10** (Step Over) and move the script one step at a time.

Variables

Let us see how to look for variable values

9. As you are executing one step at a time and the script has paused, put your mouse cursor on the variable "*browserWindow*", which is defined in your script. You will see the variable value.

```
ct '2 - Two' in 'adult_room' combo box
_roomComboBox.SelectedItem = this.BookingParams.UIAdult_roomComboBoxSele

ct '2 - Two' in 'child_room' combo box
_roomComboBox.SelectedItem = this.BookingParams.UIChild_roomComboBoxSele

ontrol uiButtonReset = new UITestControl(browserWindow);
nRes ▷ ⊕ browserWindow {Name [Adactln.com - Hotel Reservation System - Internet Explorer], C
nReset.SearchProperties.Add("Id", "Reset");
nReset.SearchProperties.Add("Name", "Reset");
nReset.SearchProperties.Add("Class", "reg_button");
```

Figure 13.8 – Watching variable values

10. Alternatively, select the variable 'browserWindow', right-click and select 'Add Watch'. You will then see this variable in the Watch window.

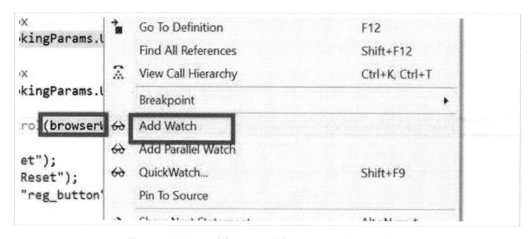

Figure 13.9 – Adding variables to a watch window

11. Expand the **browserWindow** node and all the properties of this variable will display.

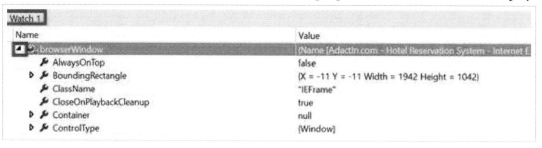

Figure 13.10 – Expanding variables to observe its properties and their values

12. Finish the script by clicking on the **Continue** icon. Save the script.

Exercise

1. Use script debugging in the parameterization project. Try to use breakpoints and watch functionality to read values from the DataFile.csv file.

಄

14.

Exception Handling in Coded UI

Introduction

We have already learned about exceptions and their handling techniques in the chapter on Basics of C#. An *exception* is an event which occurs during the execution of a program that disrupts the normal flow of the program's instructions.

Exception handling in Coded UI is also a crucial exercise. Most of the time when a Coded UI script fails, it is because it has landed into an exception. The cause could be anything like:

- Element not found
- Couldn't click the element
- Element not visible

The moment the script comes across an exception it will halt the test. So it's important for a tester to foresee these exception conditions and handle them according to the script or test requirements. This way the script failures are attributed to failures of test conditions and not to unhandled code exceptions. So, we have a bug corresponding to every test failure-which is our ultimate goal.

To catch an exception we first put the code which we suspect will throw an error into a **try** block like

```
Try
{
BrowserWindow browserWindow = new BrowserWindow();
Image imgScreenshot = browserWindow.CaptureImage();
imgScreenshot.Save("C:/scripts/popupdialog.jpg");
browserWindow.PerformDialogAction(BrowserDialogAction.Ok);
Console.WriteLine("Popup dialog appeared.");
}
catch (Exception)
```

```
{

Console.WriteLine("Popup dialog did not appear.");

Playback.PlaybackSettings.ContinueOnError = true;

}
```

Table 14.1 – Insert exception block

This is followed by a **catch block** of code where we tell the system what should be done when the exception occurs. Generally this is where we display the message of the exception object so that we know which exception has occurred and why.

In this chapter we will learn how to perform exception handling in Coded UI scripts.

Key objectives:

- Handling Coded UI Exceptions
- UITestException Class

14.1 Handling Coded UI Exceptions

In Coded UI we can use **try-catch** blocks or the **throws** statement with the purpose of handling the exceptions.

Test Scenario – If we provide an invalid username and password to the Login function, then the script should exit gracefully with a message.

Let us follow the steps to implement the above scenario.

1. **Create** a new project named **ExceptionHandlingCoded UI** under the solution MyFirstScript.

2. Copy **UIMap.uitest** from the AddWebControl project and paste into the **ExceptionHandlingCoded UI** project.

3. Update CodedUITest1.cs file in the **ExceptionHandlingCoded UI** project (see previous chapters).

4. Update namespace references in the **ExceptionHandlingCoded UI** project.

5. **Rebuild** the solution.

6. Now what visual cue tells us that a user is logged in to the application? There can be multiple visual cues but let us pick one of them being a welcome message.

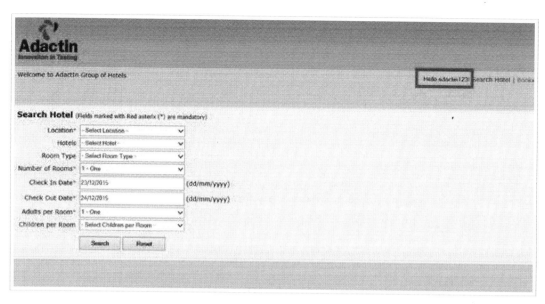

Figure 14.1 – Visual cue to validate successful login

7. Let's use Coded UI Test Builder to get its locator value. Go to the function **CodedUITestMethod1()** in **CodedUITest1.cs** file. Right-click and select **Generate Code for Coded UI Test → Use Coded UI Test Builder**.

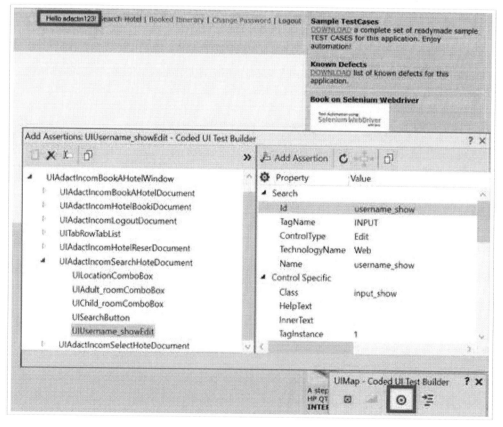

Figure 14.2 – Adding new UI Control to existing script

You see in the above snapshot the value for locator id is **username_show.**

8. Add this control to our UIMap file for further use.

> **Note:** This control might already be in your project if you have visited chapter 'Add Assertions'.

Figure 14.3 – Same control was added to script in chapter 8

9. Double-click and open UIMap.cs. Locate the Login function.

```
public void Login()
{
    #region Variable Declarations
    HtmlEdit uIUsernameEdit = this.UIAdactIncomBookAHotelWindow.UIAdactIncomHotelReserDocument.UIUsernameEdit;
    HtmlEdit uIPasswordEdit = this.UIAdactIncomBookAHotelWindow.UIAdactIncomHotelReserDocument.UIPasswordEdit;
    HtmlInputButton uILoginButton = this.UIAdactIncomBookAHotelWindow.UIAdactIncomHotelReserDocument.UILoginButton;
    #endregion

    // Go to web page 'http://www.adactin.com/HotelApp/index.php' using new browser instance
    browserWindow = BrowserWindow.Launch(new System.Uri(this.LoginParams.UIAdactIncomBookAHotelWindowUrl));
    //this.UIAdactIncomBookAHotelWindow.LaunchUrl(new System.Uri(this.LoginParams.UIAdactIncomBookAHotelWindowUrl));

    // Wait for 5 seconds for user delay between actions; Type 'adactin123' in 'username' text box
    Playback.Wait(5000);
    uIUsernameEdit.Text = this.LoginParams.UIUsernameEditText;

    // Type '{Tab}' in 'username' text box
    Keyboard.SendKeys(uIUsernameEdit, this.LoginParams.UIUsernameEditSendKeys, ModifierKeys.None);

    // Type '********' in 'password' text box
    uIPasswordEdit.Password = this.LoginParams.UIPasswordEditPassword;

    // Click 'Login' button
    Mouse.Click(uILoginButton, new Point(51, 13));
```

Figure 14.4 – Locate the Login method details in script

10. Modify the function as given below to handle a successful or unsuccessful login. The text in bold is the new code added to the Login function.

```
public void Login()

    {

#region Variable Declarations

HtmlEdit uIUsernameEdit = this.UIAdactIncomBookAHotelWindow.
UIAdactIncomHotelReserDocument.UIUsernameEdit;
```

```
HtmlEdit ulPasswordEdit = this.UIAdactIncomBookAHotelWindow.
UIAdactIncomHotelReserDocument.UIPasswordEdit;

HtmlInputButton ulLoginButton = this.
UIAdactIncomBookAHotelWindow.
UIAdactIncomHotelReserDocument.UILoginButton;

// username_show in the welcome message

HtmlEdit ulUsername_showEdit = this.
UIAdactIncomBookAHotelWindow.
UIAdactIncomSearchHoteDocument.UIUsername_showEdit;

#endregion


// Go to web page 'http://www.adactin.com/HotelApp/index.php'
using new browser instance

        browserWindow = BrowserWindow.Launch(new System.
Uri(this.LoginParams.UIAdactIncomBookAHotelWindowUrl));

//this.UIAdactIncomBookAHotelWindow.LaunchUrl(new System.
Uri(this.LoginParams.UIAdactIncomBookAHotelWindowUrl));


// Wait for 5 seconds for user delay between actions; Type
'adactin123' in 'username' text box

Playback.Wait(5000);

        ulUsernameEdit.Text = this.LoginParams.
UIUsernameEditText;


// Type '{Tab}' in 'username' text box

Keyboard.SendKeys(ulUsernameEdit, this.LoginParams.
UIUsernameEditSendKeys, ModifierKeys.None);


// Type '********' in 'password' text box

        ulPasswordEdit.Password = this.LoginParams.
UIPasswordEditPassword;


// Click 'Login' button
```

```
Mouse.Click(uILoginButton, newPoint(51, 13));


Playback.Wait(5000);

if (uIUsername_showEdit.Text.Contains(this.LoginParams.
UIUsernameEditText))

Console.WriteLine("Login Test pass for: " + this.LoginParams.
UIUsernameEditText);

else

Console.WriteLine("Login Test fail for: " + this.LoginParams.
UIUsernameEditText);



    }
```

Table 14.2 – Update script to validate successful login

11. Go to **LoginParams** class in UIMap.cs file. Modify the variable `UIUsernameEditText`. Change it to an invalid username – 'InvalidUser'.

```
public string UIUsernameEditText = "InvalidUser";
```

Figure **14.5** – Change existing script data

12. Go to CodedUITest1.cs file. If there is a method called **MyFirstAssert** within CodedUITestMethod1(), then comment it using '**//**' as shown below –

```
[TestMethod]
public void CodedUITestMethod1()
{
    this.UIMap.Login();
    //this.UIMap.MyFirstAssert();
    this.UIMap.Booking();
    // To generate code for this
}
```

Figure **14.6** – Comment the assertion method

13. Run the Test by right-clicking on the test CodedUITestMethod1() and selecting **Run Tests**

Our expectation would be that the system should print **"Login test Fail for: InvalidUser"**

14. If the script fails with "UITestControlNotFoundException" instead of throwing a valid message – as seen below

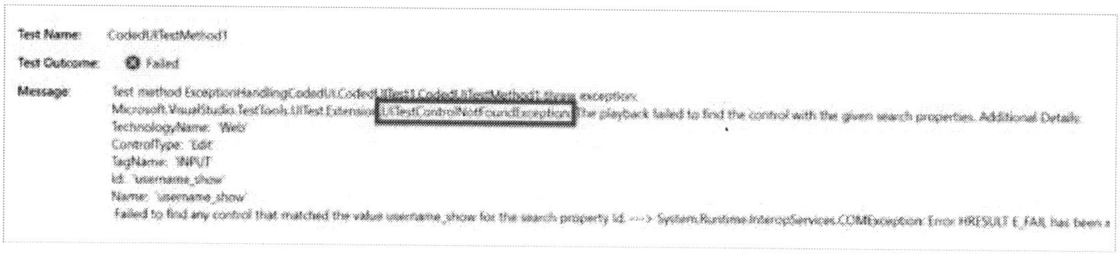

Figure 14.7 – View result of failed script

… it is because the control did not go to the else part of the condition. Whenever you try to log in using invalid user credentials,the browser will still display the login page…

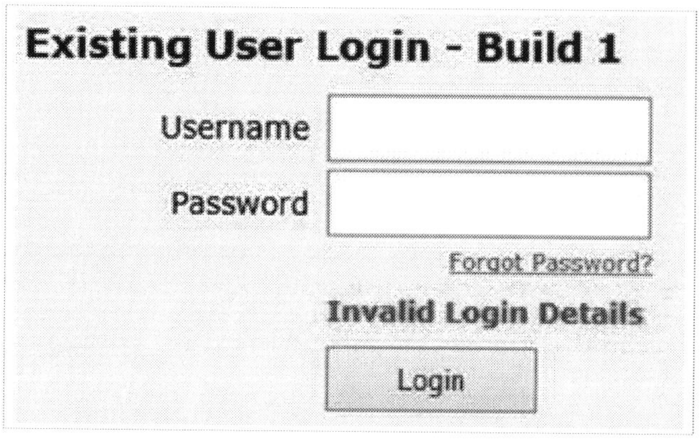

Figure 14.8 – Invalid login credentials

… while the next line of our code is looking for a page element which is displayed on the home page of the application. This leads to a **UITestControlNotFoundException** Exception and any line written after the If loop statement is not executed.

How do we resolve this gracefully?

15. We'll catch and report this exception and end the script gracefully.

Let's see the code for that

```
public void Login()

    {

#region Variable Declarations

HtmlEdit uIUsernameEdit = this.UIAdactIncomBookAHotelWindow.
UIAdactIncomHotelReserDocument.UIUsernameEdit;

HtmlEdit uIPasswordEdit = this.UIAdactIncomBookAHotelWindow.
UIAdactIncomHotelReserDocument.UIPasswordEdit;
```

```
HtmlInputButton uILoginButton = this.
UIAdactIncomBookAHotelWindow.
UIAdactIncomHotelReserDocument.UILoginButton;

// username_show in the welcome message

HtmlEdit uIUsername_showEdit = this.
UIAdactIncomBookAHotelWindow.
UIAdactIncomSearchHoteDocument.UIUsername_showEdit;

#endregion


// Go to web page 'http://www.adactin.com/HotelApp/index.php' using
new browser instance

        browserWindow = BrowserWindow.Launch(new System.
Uri(this.LoginParams.UIAdactIncomBookAHotelWindowUrl));

//this.UIAdactIncomBookAHotelWindow.LaunchUrl(new System.
Uri(this.LoginParams.UIAdactIncomBookAHotelWindowUrl));


// Wait for 5 seconds for user delay between actions; Type
'adactin123' in 'username' text box

Playback.Wait(5000);

        uIUsernameEdit.Text = this.LoginParams.
UIUsernameEditText;


// Type '{Tab}' in 'username' text box

Keyboard.SendKeys(uIUsernameEdit, this.LoginParams.
UIUsernameEditSendKeys, ModifierKeys.None);


// Type '********' in 'password' text box

        uIPasswordEdit.Password = this.LoginParams.
UIPasswordEditPassword;


// Click 'Login' button

Mouse.Click(uILoginButton, newPoint(51, 13));
```

```
Playback.Wait(5000);

try

        {

if (uiUsername_showEdit.Text.Contains(this.LoginParams.
UIUsernameEditText))

Console.WriteLine("Login Test pass for: " + this.LoginParams.
UIUsernameEditText);

else

Console.WriteLine("Login Test fail for: " + this.LoginParams.
UIUsernameEditText);

        }

catch(Exception e)

        {

Console.WriteLine(e.StackTrace);

Console.WriteLine("Login Test fail for: " + this.LoginParams.
UIUsernameEditText);

        }


    }
```

Table 14.3 – Using exception handling

In the above code we have inserted the exception prone code in a **try** block followed by a catch block to report proper results and not end poorly.

StackTrace is used to print out the program's execution stack.

When an exception is encountered and the StackTrace property is written to the console, the contents of the execution stack are printed out to standard output (i.e. command line or screen) for the developer or user to figure out which class, method and line caused the exception.

> **Note:** As in the above example, we should add Try-Catch blocks for all of our scripts and functions.

16. Now if we execute the script and look at the output, output generates a message that the Login function Failed.

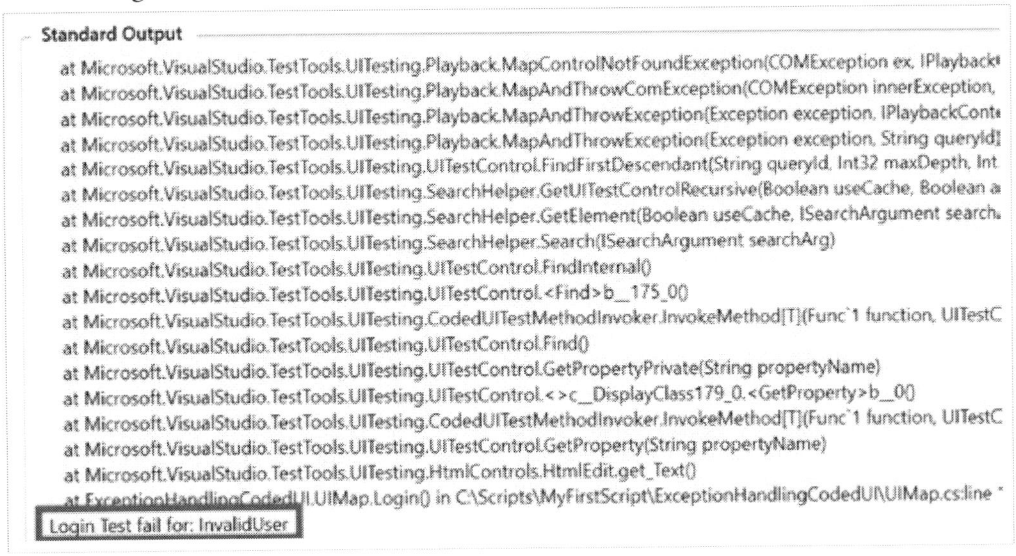

Figure **14.9** – View run results after exception handling

14.2 UITestException Class

UITestException is the parent class of all the exceptions handled by Coded UI. This base class has multiple child classes that inherit from UITestException. Find below the screenshot taken from msdn –

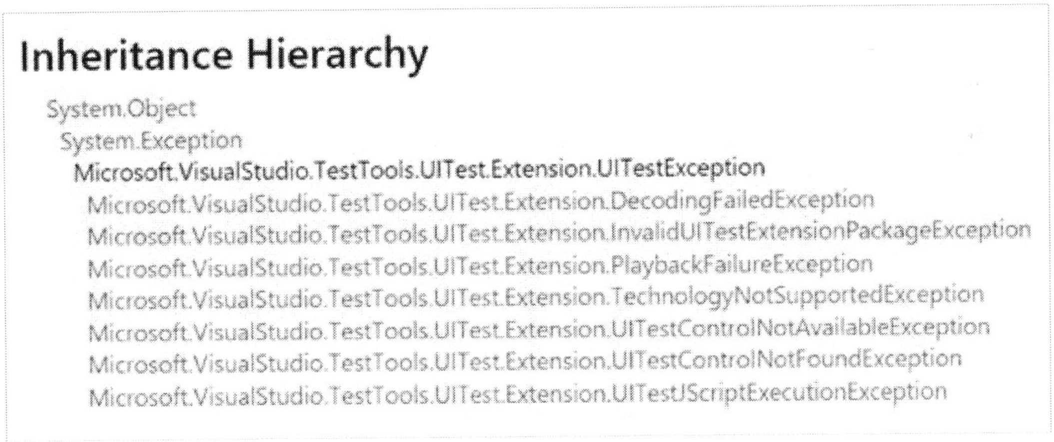

Figure 14.10 – Understand UITestException class hierarchy

Common Coded UI Exceptions

Exception Type	Description
DecodingFailedException	Thrown when a decoding operation fails because of an incorrect key file.
InvalidUITestExtensionPackage	Thrown when an invalid user interface (UI test) extension package is encountered during recording or playback.
PlaybackFailureException	Thrown when a UITestAction fails.
TechnologyNotSupportedException	Thrown when the test recording or playback is not supported on the application that is being tested.
UITestControlNotAvailableException	Thrown when the UI test framework attempts to access a UI element that is no longer available or cannot be accessed.
UITestControlNotFoundException	Thrown when the user interface (UI) test framework attempts to access a UI test control that cannot be found.
UITestJScriptExecutionException	Thrown when any javascript error occurs.

Table **14.4** – Methods available for UITestException class

> **Note:** You can find more on UITest.Extension namespace at https://msdn. microsoft.com/en-AU/library/microsoft.visualstudio.testtools.uitest. extension.aspx

Exercise

1. Add Try-Catch Blocks for all the functions we have created so far (if they do not already have Try-Catch Blocks), specifically

   • Booking()

2. Add a breakpoint at the *Console.WriteLine(e.StackTrace)*step and verify the code gets into the Catch Block by running the script in Debug mode.

 භ

15.

Working with multiple browsers

Coded UI tests can automate testing for web applications by recording your tests using Internet Explorer. These tests can then be customized and played back using either Internet Explorer or other browser types for these web applications. In this chapter, we will understand how to achieve this.

Introduction

Web-based solutions have become popular in the past few years because they provide easy access to users all around the world. Users also like them because of their convenience. Users don't need to install a separate application. With browsers alone they can connect to their accounts from any device connected to the Internet. However, for both software developers and testers, the fact that a user can choose any Web browser presents a problem—you must test a solution against multiple browsers.

In this chapter we will learn how to execute Coded UI scripts using different browsers.

Key objectives:

- "Microsoft Coded UI" – Text size is too small compared to the other text
- Executing tests in Chrome and Firefox

15.1 Installing Microsoft Coded UI components

You must use the Coded UI Test Builder to record your web application test using Internet Explorer. Cross-browser testing libraries do not ship with Visual Studio out of the box, rather, they must be downloaded as an extension from Visual Studio *Extensions and Updates*.

Installing Microsoft Coded UI components

1. On the **Tools** menu in Visual Studio, choose **Extensions and Updates**.

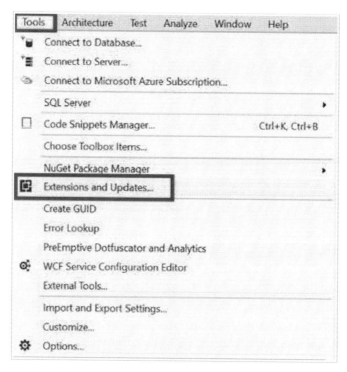

Figure 15.1 – Adding extensions

2. In the Extension and Updates dialog box, search for **Selenium components for Cross Browser Testing**. If you are able to see the extension, click on **Download**, otherwise go to step 3.

3. If you are not able to find the selenium component, download it from here - https://visualstudiogallery.msdn.microsoft.com/11cfc881-f8c9-4f96-b303-a2780156628d

4. After downloading the installer, double-click the installer and you will see the below screen -

Figure 15.2 – Installing Selenium Components

5. Continue with installing the extension. On the second screen, you need to check the option 'Add Firewall Exception for Chrome Driver' as shown below –

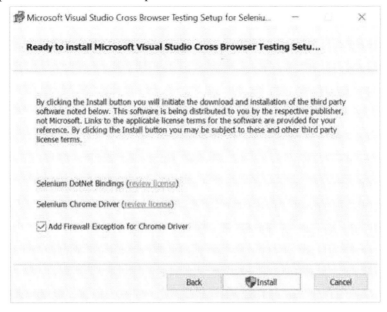

Figure 15.3 – Completing the installation

6. After installing the cross-browser testing installer, verify that Microsoft.VisualStudio.TestTools.UITest.Extension.CrossBrowserProxy.dll is found in the following location:

- *"%ProgramFiles%\Common Files\microsoft shared\VSTT\Cross Browser Selenium Components" (for 32 bit machines)*

- *"%ProgramFiles(x86)%\Common Files\microsoft shared\VSTT\Cross Browser Selenium Components" (for 64 bit machines)*

Figure 15.4 – Verifying successful install

15.2 Executing Coded UI Tests in Chrome & Firefox

> **Note:** You cannot record coded UI tests using Google Chrome or Mozilla Firefox browsers.

Once we have installed the required Selenium components, our script can be executed in Chrome or Firefox. To make the necessary changes, let us create a new project.

Let us follow the steps to implement the above scenario.

1. **Create** a new project named **CrossBrowserCodedUI** under the solution MyFirstScript.

2. Copy **UIMap.uitest** from the **AddWebControl** project and paste into the **CrossBrowserCodedUI** project.

3. Update CodedUITest1.cs file in the **CrossBrowserCodedUI** project (see previous chapters).

4. Update namespace references in the **CrossBrowserCodedUI** project.

5. **Rebuild** the solution.

6. Open UIMap.cs file.

7. In the Login() method, we have written the following code –

```
browserWindow = BrowserWindow.Launch(new System.Uri(this.LoginParams.
UIAdactIncomBookAHotelWindowUrl));
```

Table 15.1

8. In the above code, we are launching our test URL. By default, the URL is launched in Internet Explorer. To explicitly launch the test URL in Chrome, we will set the **CurrentBrowser** property of **BrowserWindow** to 'chrome'. Our updated code will look like below –

```
BrowserWindow.CurrentBrowser = "chrome";


browserWindow = BrowserWindow.Launch(new System.Uri(this.LoginParams.
UIAdactIncomBookAHotelWindowUrl));


browserWindow.Maximized = true;
```

Table 15.2 – Updating script to run in Chrome browser

9. Save the project. Run the script now.

10. You will observe that the script opens up a chrome browser and executes the script successfully.

11. To execute the same test in Firefox, change the script as shown below –

```
BrowserWindow.CurrentBrowser = "firefox";


browserWindow = BrowserWindow.Launch(new System.Uri(this.LoginParams.
UIAdactIncomBookAHotelWindowUrl));


browserWindow.Maximized = true;
```

Table 15.3 - Updating script to run in Firefox browser

Note: Apple's Safari web browser is not supported.

Support for new Browser Versions

Each browser has its own release cycle. If there is a new version that does not work with the binaries downloaded with the downloaded Selenium components, you can try the steps below and see if it fixes your issue.

1. Navigate to http://selenium-release.storage.googleapis.com/index.html and navigate into the folder for latest version

2. Download selenium-dotnet-strongnamed-<version>.zip

3. Right click on the downloaded Zip -> Properties -> General Tab -> Click UnBlock in the Security section -> OK

4. Unzip the file and copy files from net40 directory to "%programfiles(x86)%\
Common Files\Microsoft Shared\VSTT\Cross Browser Selenium Components"

5. If you are having issues with Chrome browser, you will also need to download the latest chromedriver from http://chromedriver.storage.googleapis.com/index.html , unblock the zip and copy the exe to the same directory.

Exercise

1. Execute all the scripts from prior projects in Chrome and Firefox.

✂

16.

Test Settings and Playlist Files

Introduction

When you run tests from Visual Studio or in the build service, the test framework can collect data such as diagnostic trace information, system information, or a video recording of a coded UI test. To utilize these capabilities, we use the **.testsettings** file in our projects. These diagnostics can be used to simulate potential bottlenecks on the test machines, reduce the available system memory, or emulate a slow network.

As suggested on MSDN, Test Settings file is used in the following scenarios –

- Collect diagnostic data to help isolate bugs in your application.
- Emulate potential bottlenecks that your app might occasionally encounter in a production environment.
- Run the client, server, and other parts of your app on different machines, to verify that it behaves as expected in a distributed environment.
- Distribute a large number of tests across additional machines.
- Run web performance and load tests.

You can create and save a list of coded UI tests that you want to run or view as a group. To achieve that we create a **playlist** file. This is used if you want to separate your tests based on workflows, test suites or product modules.

In this chapter we will learn how to utilize testsettings and playlist files to execute Coded UI scripts.

Key objectives:

- Adding a testsettings file
- Features of a Test Settings
- Using a Playlist

16.1 Adding a testsettings file

1. To add a testsettings file, right-click on the solution **MyFirstScript** and go to **Add → New Item**.

Note: Right click on Solution and not the project.

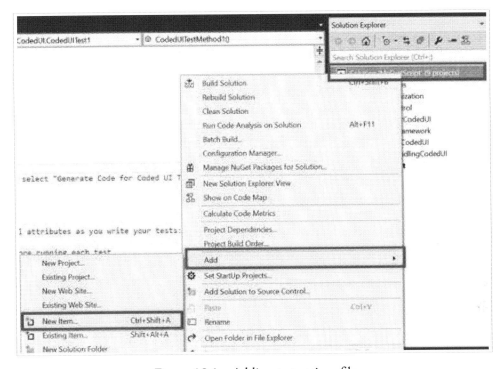

Figure **16.1** – Adding testsettings file

2. Now, select Test Settings on the left hand side menu. Select Test Settings File and name it **MyTestSettings.testsettings**. Click the **Add** button.

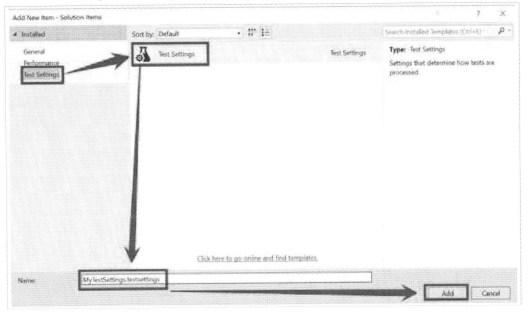

Figure **16.2** – Provide name to testsettings file

3. Once you click on the Add button, you will be shown the test Settings dialog. Click the **Close** button.

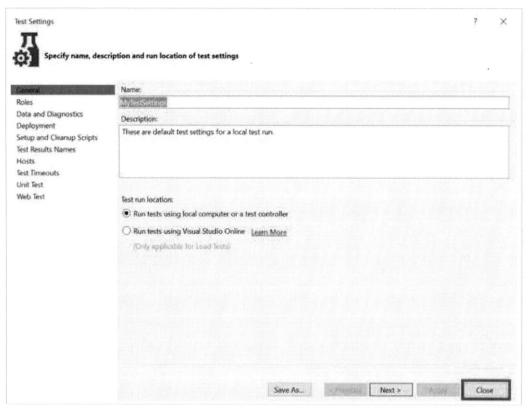

Figure **16.3** – TestSettings file dialog

4. We have now added a MyTestSettings.testsettings file to the solution. We can add more than one test settings file if we want to switch quickly between different settings. Now we need to link this file with our project. To do that go to **Test**→**Test Settings** → **Select Test Settings File**.

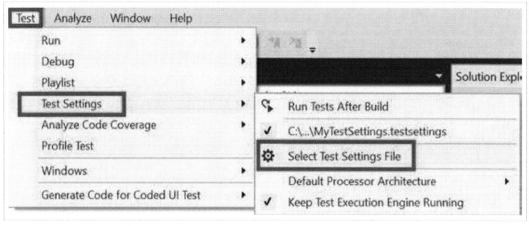

Figure **16.4** – Link testsettings file to your project

5. Go to your project location, select the **MyTestSettings.testsettings** file, and click the **Open** button.

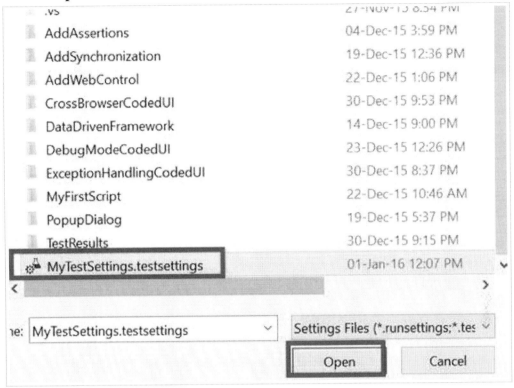

Figure 16.5 – Locate the recently created testsettings file

16.2 Features of a Test Settings file

In this section, we will briefly go through different features of a Test Settings file. To start, let us open the **MyTestSettings.testsettings** file. To do that, double-click on the file from the solution –

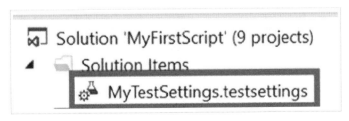

Figure 16.6 – Open testsettings file

Once you open the Test Settings it would look like below. You can observe different properties listed on the left hand side –

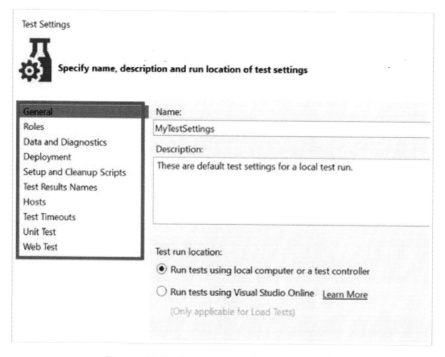

Figure **16.7** – Properties of testsettings file

Let us now look at the different properties of Test Settings.

General –

This section contains the name and description of the test settings file. We can also use Visual Studio online for web performance and Load test execution.

Roles –

On the Roles page, you can either configure the test to run on your local machine or to run remotely:

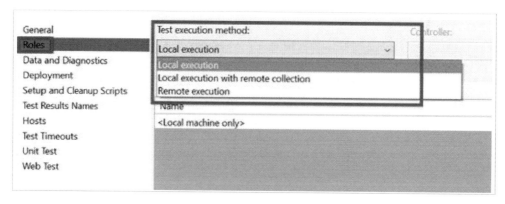

Figure **16.8** – Roles property

- Local execution is the default. It means that the tests and the application run on your Visual Studio machine, or on the build server after you have checked in the code.

- Local execution with remote collection is a typical configuration for testing a web app or client-server system. The test code runs on the local machine, but you can also collect test data from the components of the application that are installed on other machines.

- Remote execution is used where you do not want to run any part of your application locally. This is a typical configuration where the application requires particular platforms, such as a specific web browser or database. You can collect test data and configure the test environment on each machine.

> **Note:** For remote execution, a controller is required. You can either install the test controller and agents manually or you can use Microsoft Test Manager to create a lab environment.

Data and Diagnostics

To include the data and diagnostics that you want to collect on your local machine, select the diagnostic data adapters according to your testing needs. Data and diagnostics can also be collected on remote machines by specifying the roles configured in the Roles section.

By default, we can see a list of roles as shown below, with an option to enable them by checking the check-box.

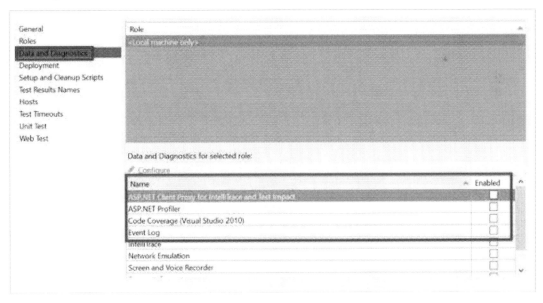

Figure 16.9 – Data and Diagnostics property

Let us briefly go through these roles –

Diagnostic data adapter
ASP.NET Client Proxy for IntelliTrace and Test Impact: This proxy allows you to collect information about the http calls from a client to a Web server for the IntelliTrace and Test Impact diagnostic data adapters.
IntelliTrace: You can configure the diagnostic data adapter for IntelliTrace to collect specific diagnostic trace information to help isolate bugs that are difficult to reproduce. This adapter creates an IntelliTrace file with an extension of .iTrace, that contains this information. When a test fails, you can create a bug. The IntelliTrace file that is saved with the test results is automatically linked to this bug. The data that is collected in the IntelliTrace file increases debugging productivity by reducing the time that is required to reproduce and diagnose an error in the code. From this IntelliTrace file the local session can be simulated on another computer, this reduces the possibility of a bug being non-reproducible.
ASP.NET Profiler: You can create a test setting that includes ASP.NET profiling, which collects performance data on ASP.NET Web applications.
Code Coverage (Visual Studio 2010): You can create a test setting that includes code coverage information that is used to investigate how much of your code is covered by tests.
Event Log: You can configure a test setting to include event log collecting, which will be included in the test results.
Network Emulation: You can specify that you want to place an artificial network load on your test using a test setting. Network emulation affects the communication to and from the machine by emulating a particular network connection speed, such as dial-up.
System information: A test setting can be set up to include the system information about the machine that the test is run on.
Test impact: You can collect information about which methods of your applications code were used when a test case was running. This information can be used together with changes to the application code made by developers to determine which tests were impacted by those development changes.

> **Screen and Voice Recorder:** You can create a video recording of your desktop session when you run an automated test. This video recording can be useful to view the user actions for a coded UI test. The video recording can help other team members isolate application issues that are difficult to reproduce.

Deployment

To create a separate directory for deployment every time that you run your tests, select **Enable deployment.**

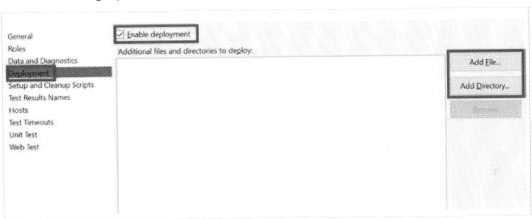

Figure 16.10 – Deployment property

To add an important file to the directory you are using for your test, click the **Add File...** button and then select the file that you want to add. To add a directory to the directory you are using for your tests, click the **Add Directory...** button and then select the directory that you want to add.

Setup and Cleanup Scripts

Here you can enter the path to your setup and cleanup scripts that need to be executed before and after executing the Coded UI scripts.

Test Results Names

Here you can define the name of the folder that will contain your test results.

Hosts

Here you can choose hosts for your tests to run. For maximum flexibility, you should compile your test projects with the Any CPU configuration. Then your scripts can run on both 32- and 64-bit agents.

Test Timeouts

This is used to limit the period of time for each test run and individual tests. To abort a test run when a time limit is exceeded, select **Abort a test run if the total time exceeds** and then type a value for this limit. To fail an individual test if a time limit is exceeded, select **Mark an individual test as failed if its execution time exceeds**, and type a value for this limit.

Unit Test

This option is used if you have to specify assembly locations that your unit tests need to load.

Web Test

This option is used to configure properties that control how **Web performance tests** are run in the test setting.

16.3 Using a Playlist

In this section we will learn how to group the tests together. To accomplish this, we will employ the Playlist concept. We can create and save a list of tests as a group. When you select a playlist, the tests in the list are displayed in the **Test Explorer** window. If not already open, then open the Test Explorer window by selecting **Test →Windows →Test Explorer**.

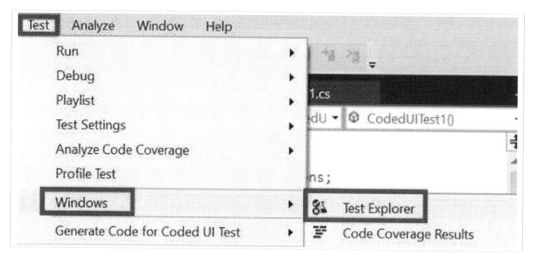

Figure 16.11 – Test Explorer Window

To create a Playlist, go to the Test Explorer window and select any test script as shown below. Then, right-click on the test and select **Add to Playlist →New Playlist**.

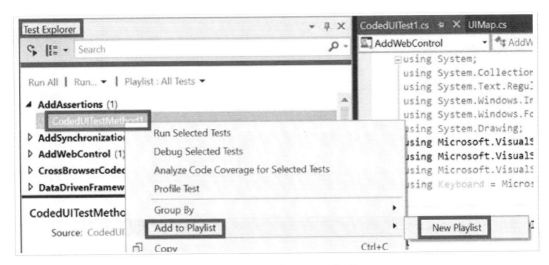

Figure **16.12** – Creating playlist

When you click on New Playlist, you will get a windows explorer dialog. You can then enter the playlist name as **MyPlaylist** and click the **Save** button.

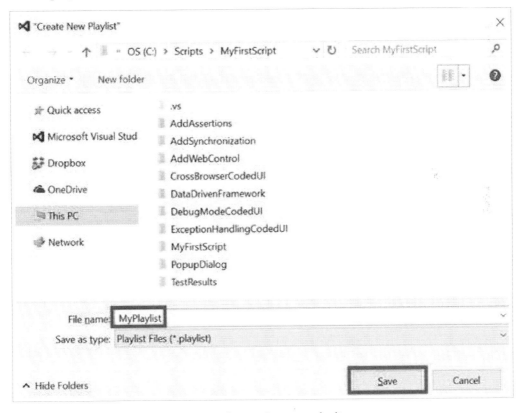

Figure 16.13 – Saving a playlist

Once we have created the playlist, we can add the test scripts to the same playlist, or create a new playlist.

Some examples where we would want to create playlist –

- Smoke Test Suite
- Regressions Test Suite
- Different Application Modules
- Workflow based
- Specific defect playlist
- Performance Test Suite

To open a playlist, choose **Test →Playlist** from the Visual Studio menu. As seen in the image below, we have two playlists: *testpl* and *MyPlaylist*.

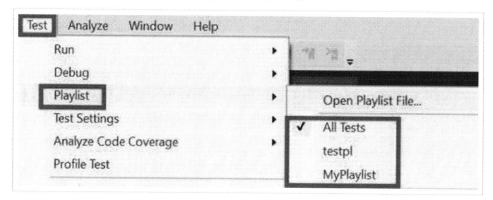

Figure 16.14 – Opening a custom playlist

Exercise

1. Use testsettings file to deploy your Coded UI scripts on a remote server.
2. Use Playlist file to group your test scripts.

℘

17.

Continuous Integration with Team Foundation Server

Introduction

Why do we need Continuous Integration tools for test automation?

Continuous Integration (CI) tools assist in creating frequent builds (usually on a daily basis) and running developer driven tests (unit tests) to provide timely feedback on application quality.

We can integrate our Coded UI based functional test automation scripts with CI tools to execute our scripts as soon as a new build is created which will provide instant feedback on application issues.

Popular open source tools include Hudson, Jenkins (the offspring of Hudson), CruiseControl and CruiseControl.NET.

Popular continuous integration tools include Microsoft's Team Foundation Server, ThoughtWorks' Go, Jetbrains' Team City, Hudson, Jenkins and Cruise Control.

As part of this chapter we will learn how Coded UI scripts integrate with Team Foundation Server, one of the popular CI tools provided by Microsoft.

About Team Foundation Server

Team Foundation Server (commonly abbreviated to TFS) is a Microsoft product which provides source code management (either via Team Foundation Version Control or Git), reporting, requirements management, project management (for both agile software development and waterfall teams), automated builds, lab management, and testing and release management capabilities. It covers the entire application lifecycle. TFS can be used as a back end to numerous integrated development environments but is tailored for Microsoft Visual Studio and Eclipse (on Windows and non-Windows platforms).

Key objectives

- Team Foundation Server 2015
- Code Repository

- Setting up build definition
- Microsoft Test Manager

17.1 Team Foundation Server 2015

We will start with downloading Team Foundation Server 2015. To do this, go to the url - https://www.visualstudio.com/products/tfs-overview-vs.

1. We will then click the Download button in the middle of the web page.

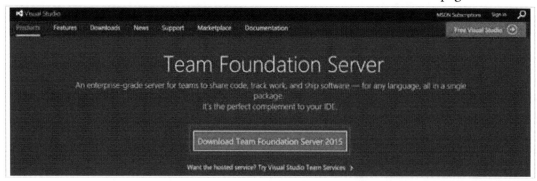

Figure **17.1** – Download page of TFS

2. Once installed, open Team Foundation Server Administration Console as shown below –

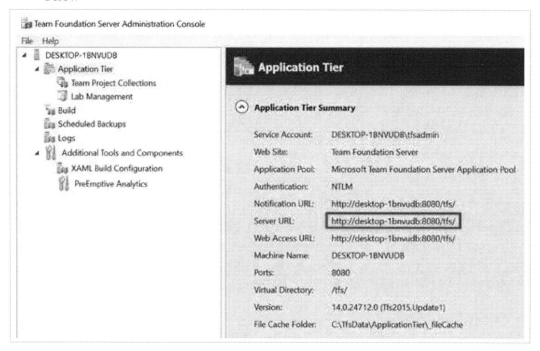

Figure 17.2 – Homepage of TFS Administration Console

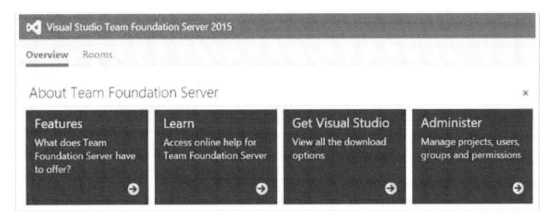

Figure 17.3 – Homepage of TFS Server

3. As highlighted in the image above, you will find the web url in which to access the TFS server. Let us use this url (http://desktop-1bnvudb:8080/tfs/) in a browser window. Once you open this url, you will observe that TFS Server is displayed.

Team Foundation Server provides version control, tools for agile teams and continuous integration (build, validate and deploy) using this url.

17.2 Code Repository

The team members of a project can be at different locations. They require a common repository for storing their work. We have 2 options for source control i.e. Git (Distributed Version Control) or Team Foundation Version Control. Any of these source control mechanisms can integrate with multiple IDEs like Visual Studio or Eclipse. We can provide security for the team by creating groups.

The code being developed can be for various Microsoft platforms like Windows, Windows Phones, Desktop or Web. Once the functionality is ready, we can check the code into Team Foundation Server directly from Visual Studio IDE. We will create a collection of artifacts in Team Foundation Server's Administration Console and link our Coded UI scripts to this collection. An example of a collection is depicted below –

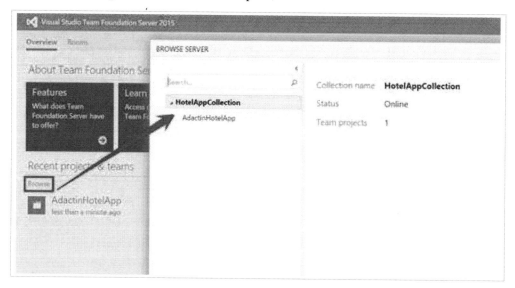

Figure 17.4 – Browse Coded UI solution from TFS Server

1. Now, open your Coded UI solution in Visual Studio.

2. Once your solution and its projects are opened in Solution Explorer, right-click on the solution and select **Add Solution to Source Control**.

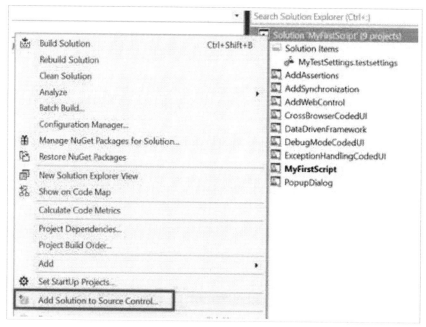

Figure 17.5 – Adding your solution to TFS

3. Once this is done a pop-up window opens up where you need to add your Source Control server details.

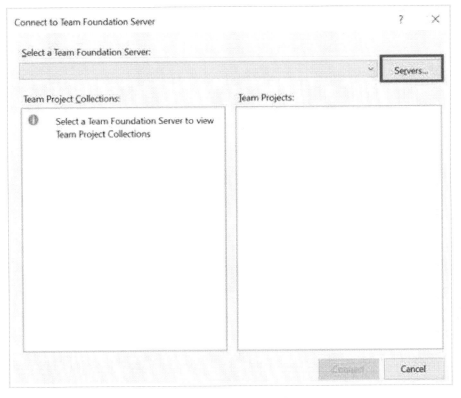

Figure 17.6 – TFS dialog

4. Now click the **Servers...**button

5. Click the **Add** button. Here you need to provide your Team Foundation Server details. Also provide the team collection name and the local code path.

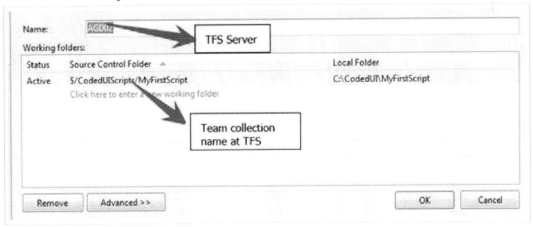

Figure 17.7 – Add TFS Server details

6. Now your Coded UI solution is connected to the Team Foundation Server. Go to Source Control window in Visual Studio. This can be opened from **View →Other Windows →Source Control Explorer** as shown below.

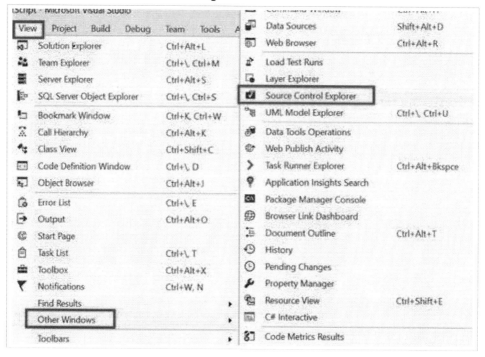

Figure 17.8 – Open Source Control Explorer window

7. In the Source Control Explorer, you will observe that your project is shown below the Team Foundation Server as shown below –

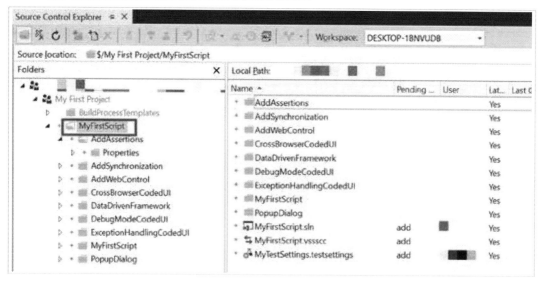

Figure 17.9 – Add solution to TFS Server

8. We now need to check-in all the Coded UI projects into the source control. To do that we need to right-click on MyFirstScript and select **Check-In Pending Changes**.

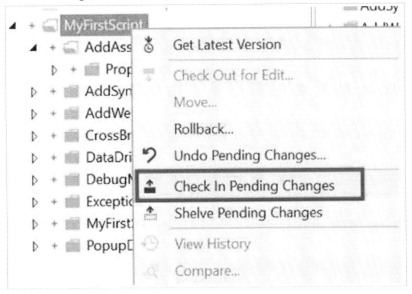

Figure 17.10 – Check-in changes to TFS Server

9. On selecting this option, you will be presented with a Team Explorer – Pending Changes window on the right hand side. By default, all files will be selected for check-in. You need to click the **Check In** button.

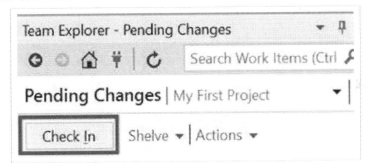

Figure 17.11 – Check-in button to save changes to TFS

10. Now all of your Coded UI projects have been pushed to the Team Foundation Server. We will verify this by going to the browser and opening the Team Foundation Server url - http://desktop-1bnvudb:8080/tfs/HotelAppCollection/AdactinHotelApp/_versionControl. If it is already opened, then refresh the web page. You will observe all of your Coded UI projects have been loaded into Team Foundation's source control.

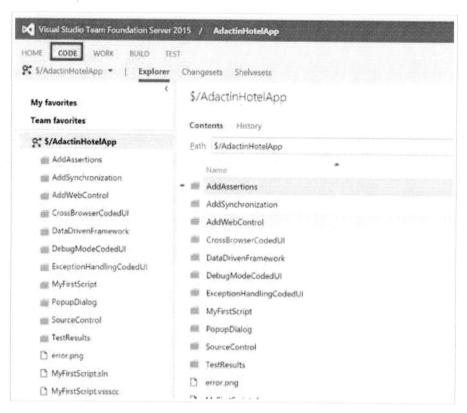

Figure 17.12 – View Code in TFS Server

This completes linking the Visual Studio project with the Team Foundation Server source control system. In the next section, we will see how we can configure build definitions.

17.3 Setting up build definition

It is a good practice to capture bugs at an early stage and also maintain the quality of the code. If we specify Continuous Integration of cloud based build services, the quality of the product can be monitored. Every time the code is checked-in, the build will be executed (configurable). The build definition needs to be created using the Build section of Team Foundation Server.

The build can be automatically triggered with each check-in. The queued build can be viewed with the **Build** tab. Once the build is completed, its information can be viewed in the **Completed** tab. Double-clicking the completed build will provide the summary. The log and diagnostics can be viewed as well. With all of these features, the build can be created with quality checkpoints.

> **Note:** The below mentioned continuous integration steps vary with projects and the type of project implementation. This activity is carried by Build Engineer or DevOps team.

To achieve this, we need to set up a build definition.

1. Go to your Team Foundation Server url.

2. Click the **BUILD** sub-tab. When you click on the **build** tab, you will get a window to create a build definition. We will select **Visual Studio** to the create build. Build definition is a stepwise process to fetch your latest code, compile your code, deploy executable files on remote servers and execute the test scripts. The build definition should look something like this –

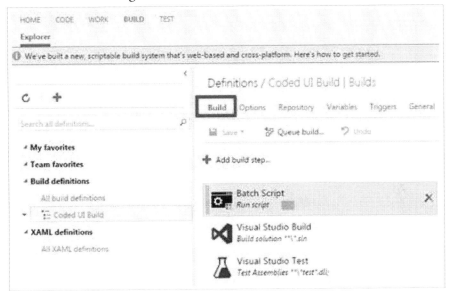

Figure 17.13 – Build tab on TFS Server

3. While performing the above step, we need to have our machines ready. The machines will be used to execute Coded UI scripts. To configure the machines in Team Foundation Server, go to **Test** →**Machines** as shown below. Here you can provide your machine details –

Figure 17.14 – Test tab on TFS Server

4. The machine details need to be provided with the build definition. You can now save the build definition.

> **Note:** You can change the name of your build definition while saving it.

5. Once the build definition is saved, we will need to perform the **Queue build** action. Click **Queue build…**

Figure 17.15 – Queue build for execution

6. On clicking Queue build, you will be asked to setup your build details. We will leave all the default options selected and click the **OK** button.

7. On clicking the **OK** button, the build process is triggered. This process will now be triggered each time you make changes to your code.

8. After few moments, you will see that the build process has completed. The build output should look like this –

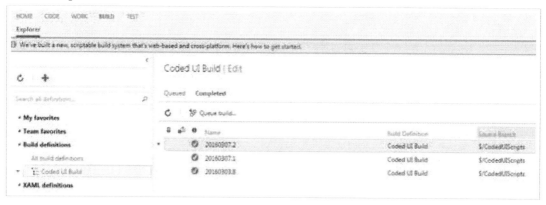

Figure **17.16** – Build successful

The above screenshot displays a successful completion of the build process. Now we have achieved Continuous Integration of our build process.

17.4 Microsoft Test Manager (MTM)

Microsoft Test Manager, the extension of Team Foundation Server and Visual Studio, allows teams to collaboratively plan, execute and track test cases and defects. Test cases, defects and other testing assets are saved in Team Foundation Server. Test suites and cases can be created in MTM and are accessible to all project team members. MTM supports Agile project methodology as well. User Stories with Acceptance Criteria or Requirements can be created and stored in MTM. All test cases can be linked to these User Stories or Requirements. This provides testing coverage and traceability.

Microsoft Test Manager comes with Visual Studio Enterprise 2015.

1. Search for, and open Microsoft Test Manager 2015 on your machine.

2. Once you open MTM, it will try to connect to the available Team Foundation Server on that machine.

3. To add a new Team Foundation Server for the first time, type the URL, or just the name of the Team Foundation Server and then choose **Add**. In our case, the MTM recognized the locally hosted Team Foundation Server.

4. We can navigate to the collection and click the **Connect now** button. This is shown below -

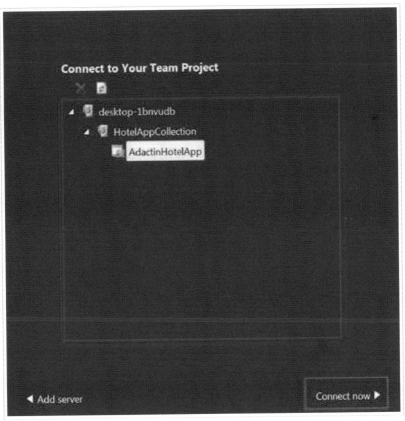

Figure **17.17** – Select TFS Collection from MTM

5. The next step is to add a Test Plan. If you do not have an existing test plan, click on the **Add** button and create a new Test Plan.

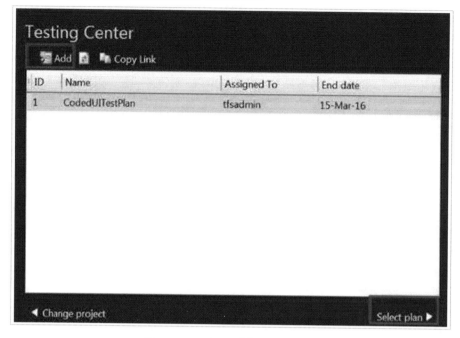

Figure 17.18 – Add a Test Plan

6. Once your plan is created, you can add a test suite and test cases within this test plan. We have created a test suite and added a test case to this test suite. This is depicted below –

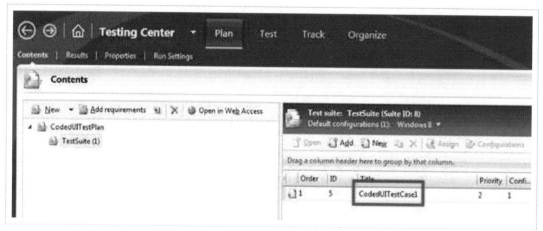

Figure 17.19 – Add a test suite

7. We now want to link our Coded UI script with this test case created in Microsoft Test Manager. You can only associate the automated test with your test case using Visual Studio. You cannot make this association using Microsoft Test Manager. If you have an existing test case that you want to use, you must first open the test case

using Visual Studio and link your test case to the Coded UI script. This is shown below –

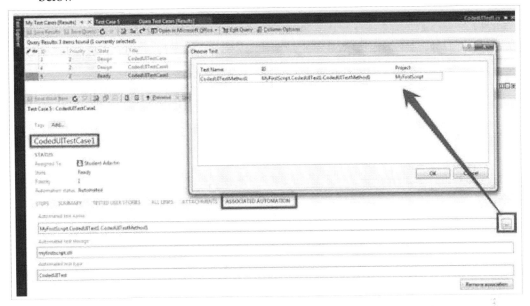

Figure 17.20 – Link Coded UI script to MTM via Visual Studio

8. Once we have done that, go to Team Foundation Server and you will be able to see the test case there. If we update our code, then the continuous integration system will fetch the code from Visual Studio, create a build and execute Coded UI script associated with the test case. The execution status of the test case can then be viewed in TFS or MTM.

Figure 17.21 – Coded UI script executed from TFS

9. We can view the status in MTM as well –

Figure 17.22 – View execution result in MTM

17.5 Advantages and Disadvantages of Continuous Integration

These are some of the advantages of continuous integration:

- You catch build breaks early on.
- In a distributed development environment where developers do not always communicate with one another, continuous integration is a great way to assure the developer that the build he or she is building is the latest one.
- Continuous integration also causes less regression
- The feedback loop is smaller.
- Integration testing moves up in the chain.
- Every check-in goes through the integration testing where problems are caught early.
- Continuous integration enforces better development processes.
- Each developer is held accountable.
- You always have a latest-and-greatest build to use in demos, showcases, etc.
- Easy integration and execution of automated scripts

On the other hand, there are some disadvantages:

- Maintenance overhead often increases.
- Some teams find that the level of discipline required for continuous integration causes bottlenecks.
- The immediate impact of a check-in often causes a backup because programmers cannot check in partially completed code.
- Specialist DevOps Engineer is required

Note: The above points are taken from MSDN (https://msdn.microsoft.com/en-us/library/ms364045(v=vs.80).aspx) and personal experiences. These might differ based on your project.

છ૭

18.

Automation Frameworks

Being a part of the software testing domain, we would have heard the term 'Automation Frameworks' many times. Again, it is a very common question one encounters at interviews too. In this chapter we will try to understand the answers to these basic questions:

- Why do we need a framework? What are the advantages of frameworks?
- What exactly is an automation framework? What are the components of the framework?
- How do we implement frameworks? What are the different types of frameworks?

18.1 Why do we need Automation Frameworks?

1. **Maintainability**

   One of the key reasons behind creating an automation framework is to reduce the cost of script maintenance. If there is any change in the functionality of the application, then we need to get our scripts fixed and working utilising the least amount of time and effort.

   Ideally, there should not be too much need to update the scripts, in case the application changes. Most of the fixes should be handled at the framework level.

2. **Productivity**

   If we ask how many manual test cases we can automate in a day that might be a difficult question to answer. But the important thing to ask is whether we can increase our productivity by automating more test cases per day?

   Yes, we can. If we have an effective framework, we can increase the productivity manifold. In one of our previous projects, we increased the productivity from 3-4 test cases a day to 10-12 test cases a day, mainly through effective framework implementation.

3. **Learning curve**

   If you have a new person joining your team, you would like to reduce the effort in training the person, and have him/her up and running on the framework as soon as possible.

   Creating an effective framework helps reduces the learning curve.

As a best practice, we always advise our clients to keep the framework as simple as possible.

4. **Make result analysis easier**

Once the test cases are automated, a lot of time is spent by the testing team on analysing the results. Sometimes they are not detailed enough, which might make it hard to pinpoint the error. Most often it is not script failure but environment or data issues that turns out to be the source of problems. A better reporting format in the framework will cut down on result analysis time considerably.

18.2 What exactly is an Automation Framework?

Frameworks are a set of guidelines which define how we will structure the various components in an automation environment. These components include object repository, test data, functions, reports and batch execution scripts.

When the development team begins development, it creates a high level design of the application. Similarly, we, as an automation team, need to create an automation framework to define how different automation components will interact with each other. We can also call it high level design for automation components.

So what are the components of the frameworks? Let us see below:

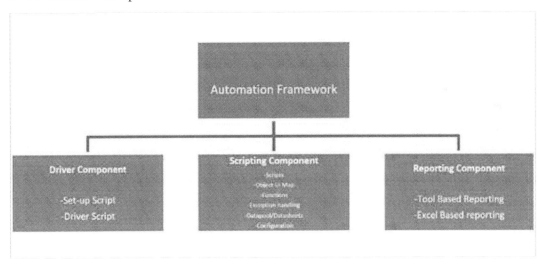

Figure 18.1 – Automation Framework

At a high level, an Automation Framework can be divided into three components:

- **Driver Component** – How will you execute the script as a batch? What setup will you need before you start execution?

- **Scripting Component** – How will you structure all of the key components of your automation framework?

- **Reporting Component** - How will you get your results?

Together, all these components make up an **Automation Framework.**

So, let us understand what exactly is stored within these components.

- **Setup Script** – This script defines what setup you need before you can start script execution

Example

In one of our projects, we had to install the new desktop thick client application, before we could kickoff the automation test execution. So we created a setup script to download the latest thick client and install it on the test machines to setup the environment.

- **Driver Script** – Most of the time we need to run our scripts overnight. So we need a driver script which can run the scripts as a suite (one after another).

- **Scripts** – These are the actual automation programs, which execute just like manual test cases

- **Shared UI Map**– A common place where all object properties and information are stored

- **Functions** – Modular programs which can be re-used across scripts

- **Configuration File** – File in which we can set up the application URL and other variable parameters in our application

- **Exception Handling**– Exception handling scenarios in our application

- **Data Pool** – Test data that will drive our scripts

- **Tool Based Reporting** – Most of the automation tools will have their own reporting format. For instance, Selenium can run tests and create TestNG or JUnit reports. Similarly in Microsoft Coded UI, results can be viewed in the MTM or TFS.

  It is also important to think about where to store these results for future reference and the ease of drilling down to the results you are looking for.

  With Coded UI we can store results in a database and read them using a custom Web based interface. This does not come with Coded UI but can be developed.

- **Excel Based Reports** – Not all tools have corresponding test management tools to store results. Quite often, and as part of a framework, the automation team has to develop their own excel drivers (at times database driven) to store results in Excel Sheets for easy viewing and analysis.

18.3 Types of Frameworks

This brings us to the next important question of how to implement frameworks and what the different types of frameworks are.

Automation developers have different reasons for following a particular framework and every framework has its own advantages and disadvantages.

We can divide frameworks into the following categories

- Level 1- Record- Replay
- Level 2- Data Driven Framework
- Level 3- Test Modularity Framework
- Level 4 - Hybrid Framework
- Level 5 - Keyword Driven Framework

We will call Level 1 the lowest level framework and Level 5 the highest.

Let's understand more about each of the different levels.

Level 1 - Record-Replay

This is not really a framework, but helps as a starting point to an introduction to frameworks.

- This framework provide the ability to capture/record the user actions and later to play them back
- Also called as Capture/Replay approach
- Enhance the recorded script with verification points, where some property or data is verified against an existing baseline
- Also note that as part of this framework, we use a shared object repository across all the scripts

Advantages

- Fastest way to generate scripts
- Automation expertise not required

Disadvantages

- Little re-use of scripts
- Test data is hard coded into the script
- New scripts always take same time to automate as previously automated scripts
- Maintenance is a nightmare

One of the key issues with this framework is that if the application workflow changes or if the test data changes, we need to go into each script and modify the script.

For instance, if you have 500 automation scripts for your application and username or password changes for your login page, you would need to go into each of the scripts and fix them, which can be a nightmare.

This leads us to our next level of framework, which resolves this issue.

Level 2 – Data Driven Framework

In this framework, while test case logic resides in test scripts, the test data is separated and kept outside the test scripts. Test data is read from the external files (Excel files, Text files, CSV files, and database) and loaded into the variables inside the test script. Variables are used both for storing input values and verification values. Test scripts themselves are prepared using the record replay approach.

Since the data is stored outside the script, if as in our previous example the username or password changes, we would need to change just one datasheet and all our 500 scripts will be fit for execution. So we avoided a huge maintenance effort using this framework.

Also we can use the same script to run multiple sets of data defined in external datasheets helping us achieve more return on investment.

Advantages

- Test data can be changed at one central place and there is no need to modify the scripts
- Changes to the Test data do not affect the Test scripts
- Test cases can be executed with multiple sets of data

Disadvantages

- If functional workflow of the application changes, it will be a maintenance nightmare
- No re-use of code

One of the key issues with the above framework is that if the workflow of the application changes, you would need to go back and fix all the scripts again.

For instance, assuming you have 500 scripts, and in each script you login to the application. Due to a new business requirement, apart from just username and password, your application now also requires your business unit name to be entered before login. This represents a change in application. Even though your data resides outside the script, you still need to go into each of the scripts and add extra lines of code to enter the business unit name. This approach is still a nightmare!

Let us look at the next level of frameworks which helps to handle this issue.

Level 3– Test Modularity Framework

As part of this framework we divide the application-under-test into libraries (Functions or Action based). These library files are then directly invoked from the test case script. This framework embodies the principle of abstraction.

In this framework, we can re-use a lot of the existing code, which helps to improve productivity.

Considering our earlier example where our login workflow has changed. We will be able to handle that issue using this framework more simplistically, as we would have created login as a separate function. This login function will be invoked from all our scripts. So we just need to add a step in the login function to enter a value in the business unit field and all our scripts should be fine.

So, as we would have understood, modular and data driven frameworks work differently; one utilizes a modular approach and the other focuses around data.

Advantages

- Higher level of code re-use is achieved in Structured Scripting compared to "Record & Playback"
- Automation scripts are less costly to develop due to higher code re-use
- Easier Script Maintenance

Disadvantages

- Technical expertise is necessary to write Scripts using Test Library Framework
- More time is needed to plan and prepare test scripts
- Test Data is hard coded within the scripts

Level 4– Hybrid Framework

In the previous section, we saw the advantages with a data driven framework and test modularity framework. Should we not get benefits of both the data driven and modular approach?

This is exactly what we do in a hybrid framework. We keep data outside our scripts and create modular functions.

Advantages

- Higher level of code re-use
- Test Data is at a central location and can be changed on demand
- Higher productivity and more scripts can be automated as we build the libraries
- Easier script maintenance

Disadvantages

- Technical expertise is necessary to write scripts and understanding of existing functions could take time
- More time is needed to plan and prepare test scripts

- Can be used by expert automation testers only

> **Note: Hybrid frameworks constitute** 80-90% of the frameworks, which are highly successful.

Level 5– Keyword Driven Framework

Hybrid frameworks have a lot of advantages, but the disadvantage is that they get too technical. Inherently testers are not programmers and so automation gets limited to automation testers only and cannot be done by functional testers or business analysts.

Keyword driven framework makes it easier for functional testers and business analysts to be involved in automation. Let us see how.

The keyword driven or table driven framework requires the development of data tables (usually Excel Sheets) and keywords, **independent of the test automation tool** used to execute them. Tests can be designed with or without the application.

For example, instead of recording a script to login to the application, if we had an Excel Sheet to store username and password and re-use, wouldn't that be easy enough for functional testers? See table below.

Object	Action	TestData
Object Repository	**(KEYWORD)**	
uIUsernameEdit(UserName)	Set	adactin123
uIPasswordEdit(Password)	Set	Xxxxx
uILoginButton(Login)	Click	
browserWindow(Adactin.com)	Verify	Loads

But how will the script actually run?

Embedded within the back-end, there will be an intermediate component, which will translate this Excel Sheet at run time and create an automation script on the fly.

The key point to remember about this framework is that the intermediate component which will translate high level excel sheet statements written by non-programmers is the complex part and can take time. Usually we would need expert programmers to write the intermediate component.

Advantages

- Provides high code re-usability

- Test tool independent
- Independent of Application under Test (AUT), same function works for other applications (with some limitations)
- Tests can be designed with or without AUT (Application under Test)

Disadvantages

- Initial investment being pretty high, the benefits of this can only be realized if the application is considerably bigger, and the test scripts are to be maintained for a few years
- Debugging of this kind of framework can be very hard
- Test data is hard-coded within every Excel based test script, which leads to data issues
- A high level of automation expertise is required to create the keyword driven framework

Even though keyword driven framework might look like the coolest thing to work on, we have seen a lot of keyword driven frameworks fail due to their disadvantages. Most commonly, I have seen that keyword driven frameworks end up being so complicated, that it is hard for anyone to debug and isolate the problem in case the script fails.

HP Business Process Test is one of the successful keyword driven frameworks, which comes bundled with HP Quality Center/HP ALM (though you need to purchase a separate license for it.).

Personally, we prefer implementing the hybrid framework since it is simple to debug and handover to functional teams. Some of the keyword driven frameworks that we encountered or developed were too hard for the client teams to understand and they ended up not using the framework.

‹›

19.

Coded UI Functions, Common Questions and Tips

In this chapter we will try to address a few of the important Coded UI functions and other common questions and tips that can be used in Selenium.

Key objectives

- Initialize and Clean up attributes
- How to take a Screen Shot
- Keyboard and Mouse methods
- How to record Mouse hovers
- How to maximize the Browser window
- Checking an Element's Presence
- Working with drop-down combo boxes
- Working with Radio buttons
- Working with Checkboxes
- Measuring Response time for performance testing using timer

19.1 Initialize and Clean up attributes

When you create a Coded UI Project, observe the CodedUITest1.cs file. You will observe that in comments there is a **MyTestInitialize()** method that has the **TestInitialize** attribute applied to it, which tells the testing framework to call this method before any other test methods. Similarly, the **MyTestCleanup()** method has the **TestCleanup** attribute applied to it, which tells the testing framework to call this method after all other test methods have been called. Use of these methods is *optional*. The **MyTestInitialize()** method can be utilized to open the browser and launch the application under test. Similarly, **MyTestCleanup()**can be used to close the browser.

Example

Below code executes javascript and returns the Web page title

```
// Use TestInitialize to run code before running each test

[TestInitialize()]

public void MyTestInitialize()

{

    // To generate code for this test, select "Generate Code for Coded

    // UI Test" from the shortcut menu and select one of the menu items.

    // For more information on generated code, see

    // http://go.microsoft.com/fwlink/?LinkId=179463


    this.UIMap.LaunchApplication();

}


// Use TestCleanup to run code after each test has run

[TestCleanup()]

public void MyTestCleanup()

{

    // To generate code for this test, select "Generate Code for Coded

    // UI Test" from the shortcut menu and select one of the menu items.

    // For more information on generated code, see

    // http://go.microsoft.com/fwlink/?LinkId=179463

this.UIMap.CloseApplication();

}
```

Table 19.1 – Test Attributes

19.2 Keyboard and Mouse methods

Handling keyboard and mouse events are done using the .NET API's. We will be looking at the namespace **Microsoft.VisualStudio.TestTools.UITesting.** It contains Keyboard and Mouse classes that are comprised of different static methods that can be used in your code to perform keyboard and mouse functionalities.

The following are the most commonly used keyboard static methods provided by the Keyboard class:

Method	Description
PressModifierKeys(ModifierKeys)	Presses the specified modifier keys without releasing them.
PressModifierKeys(UITestControl, ModifierKeys)	Presses the specified modifier keys in the given control without releasing them.
ReleaseModifierKeys(ModifierKeys)	Releases the specified keys that were previously pressed by using the Press Modifier Keys method.
ReleaseModifierKeys(UITestControl, ModifierKeys)	Releases the specified keys that were previously pressed by using the PressModifierKeys(UITestControl, ModifierKeys) method in the given control.
SendKeys(String)	Sends keystrokes to generate the specified text string.
SendKeys(String, Boolean)	Sends keystrokes to generate the specified text string.
SendKeys(String, ModifierKeys)	Sends keystrokes to generate the specified text string.
SendKeys(UITestControl, String)	Sends keystrokes to generate the specified text string.

Table 19.2 – Keyboard class methods in Visual Studio

The following are the most commonly used mouse static methods provided by the Mouse class:

Method	Description
Click()	Clicks the default mouse button.
Click(ModifierKeys)	Clicks the default mouse button while holding the specified modifier keys.
Click(MouseButtons)	Clicks the specified mouse button.

Click(UITestControl)	Clicks the default mouse button on the specified control.
Click(UITestControl, ModifierKeys)	Clicks the default mouse button on the specified control while holding the specified modifier keys.
Click(UITestControl, MouseButtons)	Clicks the specified mouse button on the specified control.
DoubleClick()	Double-clicks the mouse button.
DoubleClick(ModifierKeys)	Double-clicks the default mouse button that has modifiers.
DoubleClick(MouseButtons)	Double-clicks the specified mouse button.
DoubleClick(UITestControl)	Double-clicks the default mouse button on the specified control.
Hover(Point)	Moves the mouse to the specified location.
Hover(UITestControl)	Pauses the mouse on the specified control.
Hover(UITestControl, Point)	Moves the mouse to the specified location that is relative to the specified control.
Move(Point)	Moves the mouse to the specified location.
Move(UITestControl, Point)	Moves the mouse to the specified location that is relative to the specified control.
MoveScrollWheel(Int32)	Scrolls the mouse wheel the specified number of times.

MoveScrollWheel(Int32, ModifierKeys)	Scrolls the mouse wheel the specified number of times while pressing the specified modifier keys.
MoveScrollWheel(UITestControl, Int32)	Scrolls the mouse wheel on the specified control the specified number of times.
StartDragging()	Starts dragging the mouse.
StartDragging(UITestControl)	Starts dragging the mouse from the specified control.
StartDragging (UITestControl, MouseButtons)	Starts dragging the mouse while holding down the specified mouse buttons from the specified control.
StopDragging(Int32, Int32)	Stops the drag operation.
StopDragging(Point)	Stops the drag operation.
StopDragging(UITestControl)	Stops the drag operation on the specified control.
StopDragging(UITestControl, Int32, Int32)	Stops the drag operation on the specified control.
StopDragging(UITestControl, Point)	Stops the drag operation on the specified control.

Table 19.3 - Keyboard class methods in Visual Studio

How to use methods from Keyboard class

```
// Type 'Test Message' and Press Enter key

Keyboard.SendKeys("Test Message{ENTER}");

// Press Alt+F5

Keyboard.SendKeys("{F5}", ModifierKeys.Alt);
```

Table 19.4 – Using Keyboard class

How to use the Mouse class to drag and drop

Certain functionalities in our application need Drag and Drop. See below for a sample which uses the Mouse class to implement Drag and Drop.

```
// In this method we have a control uIToDragItem that needs to be dragged // and dropped over control uIToDropItem


Mouse.StartDragging(uIToDragItem,newPoint(17,45));

Mouse.StopDragging(uIToDropItem,newPoint(95, 11));
```

Table 19.5 – Using Mouse class

How to use Mouse class to Double-click an element

Certain functionalities in our application require a Double-click to activate the function. For example some pop-up windows will open when you double-click on them.

See below a sample code which uses the Mouse class to implement Double click

```
// Double-Click 'buttonWindow' button to open a pop-up window

Mouse.DoubleClick(uIButtonWindow,new Point(52, 5));
```

Table 19.6 – Using double-click method

19.3 How to record Mouse hovers

Under some circumstances, a particular control that's being used in a Coded UI test might require you to use the keyboard to manually record mouse hover events. For example, there might be special behavior defined for hovering over a control, such as a tree node expanding when a user hovers over it. To test circumstances like these, you have to manually notify the Coded UI Test Builder that you are hovering over the control by pressing predefined keyboard keys.

When you record your Coded UI test, hover over the control. Then press and hold Ctrl, while you press and hold the Shift and R keys on your keyboard. Release the keys. A mouse hover event is recorded by the Coded UITest Builder.

After you generate the test method, code similar to the following example will be added to the UIMap.Desinger.cs file:

```
// Mouse hover '1' label at (77, 19)

Mouse.Hover(ulItem1Text, new Point(77, 19));
```

Table 19.7 – Using mouse hover method

19.4 How to Maximize Browser Window

It is always good to maximize the browser window before you start executing your test.

Use the *Maximized* method to maximize the browser window

```
browserWindow = BrowserWindow.Launch(new System.
Uri(this.LoginParams.UIAdactIncomBookAHotelWindow
Url));

browserWindow.Maximized = true;
```

Table 19.8 – Maximize browser window

19.5 Checking an Element's Presence

Many times there will be a need to check if the Web element is present on the page. We might even want to wait some extra time to confirm whether the Web element exists on the required page. We will utilize the **TryFind()** method of web element to validate if that element exists on a page.

Example

In one of the applications we tested, it had a + icon to add bookings. But the maximum number of bookings per user was 5. So, after 5 bookings the "+" icon would disappear. One of our test cases had to verify that the "+" icon does not appear after 5 bookings. How can we verify that element exists on a page or not?

See below a sample which helps us to check whether an element exists within the stipulated timeout

```
if (uIAdditionButton.TryFind())

{

Console.WriteLine("+ icon Exist !");

}

else

{

Console.WriteLine("+ icon Does Not Exist");

}
```

Table 19.9 – Using TryFind method

We can also use **FindMatchingControls()** method, to find all the matching controls to the given web element. This method returns a collection of all UITestControls that match the specified SearchProperties and FilterProperties. This method returns UITestControlCollection. We can then search for our required control in this collection.

19.6 Working with Drop-down Combo Boxes

The Coded UI provides the HtmlComboBox class for working with Drop-down Controls. We can identify and locate these controls in a way that is similar to how we locate UI Test Controls. However, we will use the HtmlComboBox class to understand various methods for manual coding.

Look back to any of your projects. You will find this control in UIMap.cs

```
HtmlComboBox uILocationComboBox = this.
UIAdactIncomBookAHotelWindow.UIAdactIncomSearchHoteDocument.
UILocationComboBox;
```

Table 19.10 – Using HtmlComboBox class

If we want to select a value in this combo box, we can use either the mouse or keyboard to set that value. However, Coded UI utilizes the .NET methods (SelectedItem) of HtmlComboBox class to set the required value in the combo box.

Find below a few of the HtmlComboBox class methods -

Method	Purpose
ItemCount	Gets the number of items in this combo box.
Items	Gets the collection of items in this combo box.
SelectedIndex	Gets or sets the index of the selected item in this combo box.
SelectedItem	Gets or sets the selected item in this combo box.

Table 19.11 – Methods of HtmlComboBox class

Example

See below a few alternative ways of selecting location.

```
ulLocationComboBox.SelectedItem = "Sydney";
```

Or

```
ulLocationComboBox.SelectedIndex = 1;
```

19.7 Working with Radio Buttons and Groups

Using Coded UI we can select and deselect the radio buttons using the *selected()* method of the HtmlRadioButton class and check whether a radio button is selected or deselected using the *selected* method.

Look back to any of your projects. You will find this control in UIMap.cs

```
HtmlRadioButton ulRadiobutton_2RadioButton
= this.UIAdactIncomBookAHotelWindow.
UIAdactIncomSelectHoteDocument.UIRadiobutton_2RadioButton;
```

Table 19.12 – Using HtmlRadioButton class

We can select the appropriate option in the radio box using the following methods -

```
ulRadiobutton_2RadioButton.Selected = this.BookingParams.UIRa
diobutton_2RadioButtonSelected;
```

Table 19.13 – Select radio button

19.8 Working with Checkboxes

Similar to Radio Buttons we can select or deselect a checkbox using the *checked()* method of the **HtmlCheckBox** class and check whether a checkbox is selected or deselected using the *checked()* method.

```
// Select the checkbox object uiCheckBoxTest if it is present

if(uiCheckBoxTest.TryFind())

uiCheckBoxTest.Checked = true;
```

Table 19.14 – Using HtmlCheckBox class

19.9 Measuring Response time for Performance Testing using Timer

We can measure page load or response time in the Coded UI tests. We can use timers in the test code to capture the time taken for page load, rendering of the elements and JavaScript code execution.

Problem Statement – You may have noticed that when we book our hotel on Book a Hotel page by clicking on the **Book Now** button it takes some time for the page to respond. Let us see how we can find out the time it takes to book our hotel.

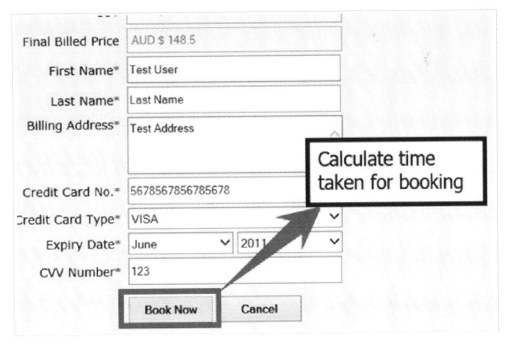

Figure 19.1 – Measure response time between steps

Logically there are three key steps we would need

- First, a way to capture timing before we click the "Book Now" button called start time

- Second, a way to notify us that the Booking has completed and the order has been generated

- Third, to capture the time again after booking, called end time, so that we can get the difference between the start and end times

How to record time

Wrapping your steps/transactions/actions in the TestContext.BeginTimer() and TestContext.EndTimer() in the CodedUI Test Method may give you a rough idea about the response times.

```
this.TestContext.BeginTimer("BooknowTimer");

Mouse.Click(ulBookNowButton, newPoint(76, 10));

this.TestContext.EndTimer("BooknowTimer");
```

Table 19.15 – Record time between steps

To view the output, after running the script, view the Console Output of your test.

෬

Multiple Choice Questions Set-3

1. Which of the following will pause the execution of the program at the specific step?

   A. DebugPoint

   B. Breakpoint

   C. Step Into

   D. Step Out

2. Which of the following will help us get the value of the Expression in Visual Studio IDE?

   A. Variables

   B. Breakpoint

   C. Watch

   D. Commands

3. In order to handle an exception in Coded UI script which of the following can be used?

   A. OnErrorGoTo method

   B. Try-Catch blocks

   C. Switch Case statement

4. Which of the following is the parent class for all exceptions handled by Coded UI?

   A. CodedUIException

   B. UITestException

   C. System.Exception

   D. None of the above

5. Do we need to install an extension to execute Coded UI script in a Chrome browser?

   A. Yes

   B. No

   C. Cannot be done

6. Which browser is not supported by Coded UI?

    A. Chrome

    B. Firefox

    C. Safari

    D. Internet Explorer

7. Which of the below is a way to Batch execute our Coded UI scripts?

    A. .testsettings file

    B. Hand coding

    C. Master scripting call to other scripts

    D. Playlist file

8. Team Foundation Server is an example of a

    A. Continuous Integration Tool

    B. Test Management Tool

    C. Performance Testing Tool

    D. Configuration Management Tool

9. Which Keyboard Class method is used to perform 'Alt+F' command?

    A. Keyboard.SendKeys("F","Alt")

    B. Keyboard.SendKeys("Alt+F")

    C. Keyboard.SendKeys(ModifierKeys.Alt, "F")

    D. Keyboard.SendKeys("F",ModifierKeys.Alt)

10. How can we record time in between two steps in Coded UI?

    A. Using TestContext.BeginTimer() and TestContext.EndTimer() methods

    B. Using TestContext.BeginTime() and TestContext.EndTime() methods

    C. Using TestClass.BeginTimer() and TestClass.EndTimer() methods

    D. Using TestClass.BeginTime() and TestClass.EndTime() methods

Answers

Q1. Answer: B

Explanation – A Breakpoint will pause the execution of a program at a specific step at which it is inserted

Q2. Answer: C

Explanation – A Watch is used to return the value of an Expression

Q3. Answer: B

Explanation – Try Catch blocks are used to catch any exceptions thrown by the Coded UI scripts

Q4. Answer: B

Explanation – In Coded UI, UITestException is the parent class for all exceptions

Q5. Answer: A

Explanation – Selenium components need to be installed from Visual Studio gallery

Q6. Answer: C

Explanation – Apple's Safari browser is not supported by Coded UI

Q7. Answer: D

Explanation – Playlist file is used to group your Coded UI scripts

Q8. Answer: A

Explanation –Team Foundation Server is an example of a continuous integration tool

Q9. Answer: D

Explanation – The method in Keyboard class is SendKeys(String, ModifierKeys)

Q10. Answer: A

Explanation – BeginTimer() and EndTimer() methods are exposed by TestContext to record time

20.
Sample Naming and Coding Conventions

20.1 Sample Naming Conventions

Standardized naming and coding conventions ensure that automation components including names of scripts, functions, Web elements and variables are consistent throughout our framework. This reflects good coding practice and assists in code maintenance later on. Generally two forms of naming conventions are followed –

- **Pascal casing:** the first character of all words is upper case and the other characters are lower case.

- **Camel casing:** the first character of all words, except the first word, is upper case and other characters are lower case.

In C#, we mostly follow Pascal casing as described in the table below –

Identifier	Casing	Example
Namespace	**Pascal**	namespace System.Security { ... }
Type	**Pascal**	public class StreamReader { ... }
Interface	**Pascal**	public interface IEnumerable { ... }

Method	**Pascal**	public class Object {
		public virtual string ToString();
		}

Property	**Pascal**	public class String {
		public int Length { get; }
		}

Event	**Pascal**	public class Process {
		public event EventHandler Exited;
		}

Field	Pascal	public class MessageQueue {
		public static readonly TimeSpan InfiniteTimeout;
		}
		public struct UInt32 {
		public const Min = 0;
		}

Enum value	Pascal	public enum FileMode {
		Append,
		...
		}

Parameter	Camel	public class convertValue {
		public static int toInt32(string value);
		}

Table 20.1 – Pascal notation

1. **Automation components naming convention** – You can follow these naming conventions for automation components

Subtype	Syntax	Example
Tests	[Product]_ [TestCaseID]_ [TestType]_ [Test Name]	*HA_TC101_BP_ FindHotel*
Functions	**[Product]_[FunctionType]_ [FunctionName]**	*HA_GBF_HotelBooking.cs*
Data Table	[Product]_ [DataTableType]_[Table Name]	HA_DE_FindHotel.xls
Objects	uI[Object Description][Object Type]	uISubmitButton

Table 20.2 – Naming convention

Syntax Description

- Product/Project [Product]
  - * **HA**- Hotel Application (Name of the project/product)
- TestCase ID [TestCaseID]
  - * **TC101** – Represents Testcase id TC101
- Test Types [TestType]
  - * **BP**: Business Process Script (End to end test)

* **TC**: Test Case Script (test that maps to functional test case)
* **UT**: Utility Script (test that assists as a utility script. E.g., test data creation test)
* **UI**: User Interface Script (test that validates User Interface)

- Test Name [TestName]

  * **VerifyValidLogin** – Brief description of test case objective

- Function Types [FunctionType]

  * **GBF**: Global Business Function
  * **LBF**: Local Business Function
  * **VF**: Verification Function
  * **UF**: Utility Function
  * **RF**: Recovery Function

- Function Name [Function Name]

  * **Login** – Brief description of Function Objective

- Data Table Types [DataTableType]

  * **DE**: Data Entry Data table (Datasheet used with objective of reading data from a particular row of sheet. For e.g., Login with row id 3)
  * **DL**: Data Loop Data Table (Datasheet used with objective of data driving the test with multiple data values)

- UI Map Name [UI Map Name]

  * **SharedUIMap** – Brief description of Shared UI Map

20.2 Coding Conventions

1. C# Coding Conventions

Variable Naming Convention

For purposes of readability and consistency, use Camel casing for variables and method parameters in your C# code.

```
publicclass HelloWorld

{

int totalCount = 0;

void SayHello(string name)

 {

string fullMessage = „Hello „ + name;

  ...

 }

}
```

Table 20.3 – Variable naming convention

Descriptive Variable and Procedure Names

The body of a variable or procedure name should use mixed case and should be as complete as necessary to describe its purpose. In addition, procedure names should begin with a verb, such as **InitNameArray** or **CloseDialog**.

For frequently used or long terms, standard abbreviations are recommended to help keep name length reasonable. In general, variable names greater than 32 characters can be difficult to read.

When using abbreviations, make sure they are consistent throughout the entire script. For example, randomly switching between Cnt and Count within a script or set of scripts may lead to confusion.

2. Code Commenting Conventions

Comments are an integral part of any programming language. They help maintenance engineers understand the objective of lines of code. As a good coding practice, key logic in the code should have comments.

Guidelines for Comments for Functions

Heading	Mandatory	Comment Contents
Function	Mandatory	Name of the function and the description.
Inputs	Mandatory	List of variables passed into the function as the parameters.

Outputs	Mandatory	List of variables as the output of the function.
Returns	Mandatory	List of variables returned by the function.
Usage	Optional	Specific information about how the function is implemented, and how that might affect its usage in a script.
See Also	Optional	Linking to any related topic – similar / opposite functions, type definitions.

Example:

/*

****

public static String Function: string HA_GF_readXL (**int** rownum, String columnname, String filepath)

A sample function for demonstrating comment format.

Inputs:

rownum– An integer representing the row of the Excel sheet to be read

columnname– A string used to represent the name of the column to be read

filepath– A string path of the location of the Excel file

OutPuts:

content– A String value for data read from an Excel sheet and returned by the function

Returns:

A valid String for success

Incase of failure will return an exception and message

History:

QA1   Create   Version 1.006/06/2015

QA2   Update   Version 1.107/07/2015 - Updated for error handling

Usage / Implementation Notes:

Make sure file is of extension .xls and not .xlsx

Make sure datasheet ends with extension

See Also:

<HA_GF_WriteXl>

****

*/

publicstaticstring HA_GF_readXL (**int** rownum, String columnName, String filePath)

{

// lines of code

}

☙

21.

Common Coded UI Interview Questions

We have been on interview panels for quite a few IT departments of IT consulting and non-IT companies. In ourpersonal experience, interview questions are centered on Tool technical knowledge, test automation experience, scenario and approach based techniques, which helps the interviewer judge the depth of automation experience that a candidate possesses.

This chapter discusses some of the questions we recommend that you be prepared for when you are shortlisted for Coded UI based Test Automation interviews.

21.1 Common Test Automation and Coded UI Interview Questions

- Can you explain the automation framework you have developed using Coded UI in your recent project?

Answer - Refer to our automation frameworks chapters to answer this question

- What are the key challenges you faced doing automation?

Answer - Some of the key challenges are

* Automation Environment unavailability

* Application is unstable

* Features and workflows being changed frequently leading to maintenance issues

* Test Data is changed frequently and needs regular modification and maintenance

* Objects and their properties are changed frequently

* Unreal expectations from the project manager or test manager, if they expect automation to happen at the click of a button

* Automation tool support to automate all features of an application

* Managing test results for every build for future reference

- How comfortable are you with scripting and programming (Java or C#)?
- Any scenarios in your previous projects where you had worked on maintenance of scripts? What were the challenges encountered?
- How did you decide on your selection candidates (i.e. test cases to be automated) for automation in your previous projects?

Answer – Key criteria include

* Acceptance test cases
* High priority business requirements
* Test cases which need to be executed multiple times with different sets of data
* Test environment preparation scenario
* Test cases which are complex and take a lot of time for automation
* End-to-end business processes
* Based on defects found earlier in the application

- So what automation process will you follow, if you would need to automate the application from the ground up?

Answer – Refer to *Planning Before Automation* chapter to answer this question

- How many test cases can you automate in one day?

Answer – Now this really depends on how big the test case is, the type of application you are working with, and the automation framework you are using. At a very high level, if you start without any automation framework on a Web based application and a test case with 10 steps each; you can automate up to 3-4 test cases a day. But as mentioned, it can vary a lot based on different factors and your expertise on the tool.

- What's the difference between SearchProperties and FilterProperties?

Answer – Coded UI scans through the Search properties with "AND" conditions, if all those are met, then Coded UI identifies the UITestControl. If a Search Property or a UITestControl isnot found, then CodedUI will start looking for Filter Properties with the "OR" condition.

- Why are changes in the Designer File not recommended?

Answer –Old versions of code will be over-written in the Designer file.

- How do you get properties of objects from your application, using Coded UI?

Answer – Use GetProperty() method to get a property value

- What is Mouse Class?

Answer – Refer to chapter "Coded UI Functions, Common Questions and Tips" on how to use the Mouse Class.

- What is Keyboard Class?

Answer – Refer to chapter "Coded UI Functions, Common Questions and Tips" on how to use the Keyboard Class.

- Have you integrated Coded UI scripts with any continuous Integration tool? How can we use Continuous integration tools

Answer – Refer to chapter "Continuous Integration with Team Foundation Server"

- How does Coded UI Handle Pop-up or Frames?

Answer – Refer to chapter "Handling Pop-up Dialogs and Image Capture"

- How can you read or write data to an Excel file in C# (or Coded UI)

Answer – Refer to chapter, "Data Driven Framework"

- Can you use Coded UI to perform Drag and Drop operations?

Answer – Yes, using static methods from Mouse Class. Refer to chapter "Coded UI Functions, Common Questions and Tips" on how to use the Mouse Class.

- What are the solutions if a control is not detected by Coded UI?

Answer - Refer to chapter "Working with User Interface Controls" on how to identify web controls.

- Have you executed your Coded UI scripts on multiple browsers? How?

Answer – Refer to chapter "Working With Multiple Browsers" on how to run Coded UI scripts on multiple browsers.

- How can you check if a checkbox or Radio button in your application is currently selected?

Answer – use Selected property

- How comfortable are you in debugging Coded UI scripts? What are Breakpoints, Variables, Watches used for?

Answer – Refer to chapter "Debugging Scripts"

- How do you handle exceptions in Coded UI?

Answer – Refer to chapter "Exception Handling in Coded UI"

- What are the naming conventions you follow in Coded UI?

Answer – Refer to chapter "Sample Naming and Coding Conventions"

- Give a list of tools/softwares/add-ons you have used while working with Coded UI

Answer: Key tools/software include

* .NET Framework

*   Microsoft Visual Studio
*   Microsoft Test Manager
*   Team Foundation Server
*   Microsoft Excel

ços

22.

Sample Test Cases for Automation

Test Case Id	Objective	Steps	Test Data	Expected Results
TC-101	To verify valid login Details	1. Launch hotel reservation application using URL as in test data. 2. Login to the application using username and password as in test data.	URL:http://adactin.com/HotelApp/index.php User:{test username} Password:{test password}	User should login to the application.
TC-102	To verify whether the check-out date field accepts a later date than check-in date.	1. Launch hotel reservation application using URL as in test data. 2. Login to the application using username and password as in test data. 3. Select location as in test data. 4. Select hotel as in test data.	URL: http://adactin.com/HotelApp/index.php User:{test username} Password:{test password} Location: Sydney	System should report an error message.

| | | 5. Select room type as in test data.

6. Select no-of-rooms as in test data.

7. Enter check-in-date later than the check-out-date field as in test data.

8. Verify that system gives an error saying 'check-in-date should not be later than check-out-date'. | Hotel: Hotel Creek

Room type: standard

No-of-rooms:1

Check-in-date: today + 7 date

Checkout date:today+5 date | |
| TC -103 | To check if error is reported if check-out date field is in the past | 1. Launch hotel reservation application using URL as in test data.

2. Login to the application using username and password as in test data.

3. Select location as in test data.

4. Select hotel as in test data.

5. Select room type as in test data. | URL: http://adactin. com/HotelApp/index. php

User:{test username}

Password:{test password}

Location: Sydney

Hotel: Hotel Creek | System should report an error message 'Enter Valid dates'. |

		6. Select no-of-rooms as in test data. 7. Enter check-out-date as in test data. 8. Verify that application throws error message	Room type: standard No-of-rooms:1 Check-in-date: today's -5 date Check-out date: today's -3 date	
TC-104	To verify whether locations in Select Hotel page are displayed according to the location selected in Search Hotel	1. Launch hotel reservation application using URL as in test data. 2. Login to the application using username and password as in test data. 3. Select location as in test data. 4. Select hotel as in test data. 5. Select room type as in test data. 6. Select no-of-rooms as in test data. 7. Enter check-out-date as in test data.	URL: http://adactin.com/HotelApp/index.php User:{test username} Password:{test password} Location: Sydney Hotel: Hotel Creek Room type: standard No-of-rooms:1	Location displayed in Select Hotel should be the same as location selected in search hotel form.

		8. Select No-of-adults as in test data.	Check-in-date: today's date	
		9. Select No-of-children as in test data.	Checko-ut-date:today+1 date	
		10. Click on Search button.	No-of-adults:1	
		11. Verify that hotel displayed is the same as selected in search Hotel form.	No-of-children: 0	
TC-105	To verify whether Check-in date and Check-out date are being displayed in Select Hotel page according to the dates selected in search Hotel.	1. Launch hotel reservation application using URL as in test data.	URL: http://adactin.com/HotelApp/index.php	Check-in-date and check-out-date should be displayed according to the data entered in search hotel form.
		2. Login to the application using username and password as in test data.	User:{test username}	
		3. Select location as in test data.	Password:{test password}	
		4. Select hotel as in test data.	Location: Sydney	
		5. Select room type as in test data.	Hotel: Hotel Creek	
		6. Select no-of-rooms as in test data.	Room type: standard	

		7. Enter check-out-date as in test data. 8. Select No-of-adults as in test data. 9. Select No-of-children as in test data. 10. Click on Search button. 11. Verify that check-in-date and check-out-dates are the same as selected in search hotel form.	No-of-rooms:1 Check-in-date: today's date Checkoutdate:today+1 date No-of-adults:1 No-of-children:0	
TC-106	To verify whether no. of rooms in Select Hotel page is same as the Number of rooms selected in search hotel page	1. Launch hotel reservation application using URL as in test data. 2. Login to the application using username and password as in test data. 3. Select location as in test data. 4. Select hotel as in test data. 5. Select room type as in test data.	URL: http://adactin.com/HotelApp/index.php User:{test username} Password:{test password} Location: Sydney Hotel: Hotel Creek	No-of-rooms should be displayed and match with number of rooms in search hotel page

		6. Select no-of-rooms as in test data.	Room type: standard	
			No-of-rooms:3	
		7. Enter check-out-date as in test data.	Check-in-date: today's date	
		8. Select No-of-adults as in test data.	Checkoutdate:today+1 date	
		9. Select No-of-children as in test data.	No-of-adults:1	
		10. Click on Search button.	No-of-children: 0	
		11. Verify that no-of-rooms is reflected according to the number of rooms selected in search hotel page.		
TC-107	To verify whether Room Type in Select Hotel page is same as Room type selected in search hotel page	1. Launch hotel reservation application using URL as in test data.	URL: http://adactin.com/HotelApp/index.php	Room type displayed should be the same as selected in search hotel page
		2. Login to the application using username and password as in test data.	User:{test username}	
			Password:{test password}	
		3. Select location as in test data.	Location: Sydney	
		4. Select hotel as in test data.		

| | | 5. Select room type as in test data.

6. Select no-of-rooms as in test data.

7. Enter check-out-date as in test data.

8. Select No-of-adults as in test data.

9. Select No-of-children as in test data.

10. Click on Search button.

11. Verify that room type reflected is the same as selected in search hotel page. | Hotel: Hotel Creek

Room type: Deluxe

No-of-rooms:1

Check-in-date: today's date

Checkoutdate:today+1 date

No-of-adults:1

No-of-children:0 | |
| TC-108 | To verify whether the total price (excl.GST) is calculated as "price per night * no. of nights* no of rooms". | 1. Launch hotel reservation application using URL as in test data. | URL: http://adactin. com/HotelApp/index. php | Total price =125*1*2=250$ |

		2. Login to the application using username and password as in test data.	User:{test username}
			Password:{test password}
		3. Select location as in test data.	Location: Sydney
		4. Select hotel as in test data.	Hotel: Hotel Creek
		5. Select room type as in test data.	Room type: standard
			No-of-rooms:2
		6. Select no-of-rooms as in test data.	Check-in-date: today's date
		7. Enter check-out-date as in test data.	Check-out-date:today+1 date
		8. Select No-of-adults as in test data.	No-of-adults:1
		9. Select No-of-children as in test data.	No-of-children: 0
		10. Click on Search button.	
		11. Select the hotel and click on continue button	
		12. Verify that total-price(excl. GST) is being calculated as (price-per-night*no-of-nights*no-of-rooms)	

TC-109	To verify when pressed, logout button logs out from the application.	1. Launch hotel reservation application using URL as in test data. 2. Login to the application using username and password as in test data. 3. Select location as in test data. 4. Select hotel as in test data. 5. Select room type as in test data. 6. Select no-of-rooms as in test data. 7. Enter check-out-date as in test data. 8. Select No-of-adults as in test data. 9. Select No-of-children as in test data. 10. Click on Search button. 11. Select the hotel and click on continue button.	URL: http://adactin.com/HotelApp/index.php User:{test username} Password:{test password} Location: Sydney Hotel: Hotel Creek Room type: standard No-of-rooms:2 Check-in-date: today's date Check-out-date:today+1 date No-of-adults:1 No-of-children:0	User should logout from the application.

		12. Enter the details and click on book now. 13. Click on logout and verify we have been logged out of the application.		
TC-110	To check correct total price is being calculated as "price per night*no of days*no of rooms in Book a hotel page	1. Launch hotel reservation application using URL as in test data. 2. Login to the application using username and password as in test data. 3. Select location as in test data. 4. Select hotel as in test data. 5. Select room type as in test data. 6. Select no-of-rooms as in test data. 7. Enter check-out-date as in test data. 8. Select No-of-adults as in test data.	URL: http://adactin.com/HotelApp/index.php User:{test username} Password:{test password} Location: Melbourne Hotel: Hotel Creek Room type: standard No-of-rooms:2 Check-in-date: today's date Check-out-date:today+1 date	Total-price should be calculated as (price-per-night*no-of-rooms*no-of-days Total Price= 125*2*1 = 250$ In book a hotel page

		9. Select No-of-children as in test data.	No-of-adults:1 No-of-children:0	
		10. Click on Search button.		
		11. Select the hotel and click on continue button		
		12. Verify that total-price is being calculated as (price-per-night*no-of-rooms*no-of-days + 10% GST")		
TC-111	To check Hotel name, Location, room type, Total Day, price per night are same in Booking confirmation page as they were selected in previous screen	1. Launch hotel reservation application using URL as in test data. 2. Login to the application using username and password as in test data. 3. Select location as in test data. 4. Select Hotel as in test data. 5. Select room type as in test data. 6. Select no-of-rooms as in test data.	URL: http://adactin.com/HotelApp/index.php User:{test username} Password:{test password} Location: Sydney Hotel: hotel Creek Room type: standard No-of-rooms:2	Data should be same as selected in previous screen

		7. Enter check-out-date as in test data. 8. Select No-of-adults as in test data. 9. Select No-of-children as in test data. 10. Click on Search button. 11. Select the hotel and click on continue button 12. Verify Hotel name, Location, room type, Total Day, price per night are same in Booking confirmation page as they were selected in previous screen	Check-in-date: today's date Check-out-date:today+1 date No-of-adults:1 No-of-children:0	
TC-112	To check correct Final billed price is Total Price + 10% Total price in Book a Hotel page		URL: http://adactin. com/HotelApp/index. php	Final billed Price=125+12.5 =137.5 in Book a Hotel page

		1. Launch hotel reservation application using URL as in test data.	User:{test username} Password:{test password} Location: Sydney Hotel: Hotel Creek Room type: standard No-of-rooms:2 Check-in-date: today's date Check-out-date:today+1 date No-of-adults:1 No-of-children:0	
		2. Login to the application using username and password as in test data.		
		3. Select location as in test data. Select Hotel as in test data.		
		4. Select room type as in test data.		
		5. Select no-of-rooms as in test data.		
		6. Enter check-out-date as in test data.		
		7. Select No-of-adults as in test data.		
		8. Select No-of-children as in test data.		
		9. Click on Search button.		
		10. Select the hotel and click on continue button		

		11. Verify that Final Billed Price is being calculated as (price-per-night*no-of-rooms*no-of-days		
TC-113	To verify whether the data displayed is same as the selected data in Book hotel page	1. Launch hotel reservation application using URL as in test data. 2. Login to the application using username and password as in test data. 3. Select location as in test data. 4. Select Hotel as in test data. 5. Select room type as in test data. 6. Select no-of-rooms as in test data. 7. Enter check-out-date as in test data. 8. Select No-of-adults as in test data. 9. Select No-of-children as in test data.	URL: http://adactin. com/HotelApp/index. php User:{test username} Password:{test password} Location: Sydney Hotel: Hotel Creek Room type: standard No-of-rooms:2 Check-in-date: today's date Check-out-date:today+1 date	Hotel: hotel Creek Room type: Standard No-of-rooms:2 Check-in-date:27/07/2016 Checkoutdate: 28/07/2016 No-of-adults:1 No-of-children: 0

		10. Click on Search button. 11. Select the hotel and click on continue button 12. Verify displayed data is same as the selected data in Book hotel page	No-of-adults:1 No-of-children: 0	
TC-114	Verify Order number is generated in booking confirmation page	1. Launch hotel reservation application using URL as in test data. 2. Login to the application using username and password as in test data. 3. Select location as in test data. 4. Select hotel as in test data. 5. Select room type as in test data. 6. Select no-of-rooms as in test data. 7. Enter check-out-date as in test data. 8. Select No-of-adults as in test data.	URL: http://adactin. com/HotelApp/index. php User:{test username} Password:{test password} Location: Sydney Hotel: hotel Creek Room type: standard No-of-rooms:2 Check-in-date: today's date	ORDER no should be generated

		9. Select No-of-children as in test data.	Check-out-date:today+1 date	
		10. Click on Search button.	No-of-adults:1	
		11. Select the hotel and click on continue button	No-of-children: 0	
		12. Verify Order number is generated		
TC-115	To verify whether the booked itinerary details are not editable.	1. Launch hotel reservation application using URL as in test data.	http://adactin.com/ HotelApp/index.php	Details once accepted should not be editable
		2. Login to the application using username and password as in test data.	User:{test username} Password:{test password}	
		3. Select location as in test data.	Location: Adelaide	
		4. Select Hotel as in test data.	Hotel: Hotel Cornice	
		5. Select room type as in test data.	Room type: standard	
		6. Select no-of-rooms as in test data.	No-of-rooms:2	
		7. Enter check-out-date as in test data.		

		8. Select No-of-adults as in test data. 9. Select No-of-children as in test data. 10. Click on Search button. 11. Select the hotel and click on continue button 12. Fill the form and click on Book now button. 13. Click on My itinerary button 14. Verify that the details are not editable	Check-in-date: today's date Check-out-date:today+1 date No-of-adults:1 No-of-children: 0	
TC-116	To check whether the booked itinerary reflects the correct information in line with the booking.	1. Launch hotel reservation application using URL as in test data. 2. Login to the application using username and password as in test data. 3. Select location as in test data. 4. Select hotel as in test data.	http://adactin.com/HotelApp/index.php User:{test username} Password:{test password} Location: Sydney Hotel: Hotel Creek	Itinerary should reflect the correct information in line with the booking.

		5. Select room type as in test data.	Room type: standard	
		6. Select no-of-rooms as in test data.	No-of-rooms:2	
		7. Enter check-out-date as in test data.	Check-in-date: today's date	
		8. Select No-of-adults as in test data.	Check-out-date:today+1 date	
		9. Select No-of-children as in test data.	No-of-adults:1	
		10. Click on Search button.	No-of-children: 0	
		11. Select the hotel and click on continue button		
		12. Fill the form and click on Book now button.		
		13. Click on My itinerary button		
		14. Verify that the details are reflected correctly as per the booking		

TC-117	To check whether "search order id" query is working and displaying the relevant details.	1. Launch hotel reservation application using URL as in test data. 2. Login to the application using username and password as in test data. 3. Click on booked itinerary link. 4. Enter the order id. 5. Verify that the relevant details are displayed	http://adactin.com/HotelApp/index.php User:{test username} Password:{test password} Order id :pick existing order id	Search Order ID query should display the relevant details for Order ID
TC-118	Verify that all the details of newly generated order number in booked itinerary page are correct and match with data during booking.	1. Launch hotel reservation application using URL as in test data. 2. Login to the application using username and password as in test data. 3. Book an order as in previous test cases 4. Click on My itinerary button 5. Search for Order number	http://adactin.com/HotelApp/index.php User:{test username} Password:{test password} Location: Sydney Hotel: Hotel Creek	All the details in booked itinerary page should be same as those entered during booking

		6. Verify all the details of order number are correct as entered during saving order	Room type: standard No-of-rooms:2 Check-in-date: today's date Check-out-date:today+1 date No-of-adults:1 No-of-children: 0	
TC-119	To verify that the order gets cancelled after click on Cancel order number link	1. Launch hotel reservation application using URL as in test data. 2. Login to the application using username and password as in test data. 3. Book the Hotel as in previous test cases. Keep a note of order number generated 4. Click on Booked Itinerary link 5. Search for order number booked 6. Click on Cancel <Order Number>	http://adactin.com/ HotelApp/index.php User:{test username} Password:{test password}	Order number should no longer be present in booked itinerary page after cancellation

		7. Click Yes on pop-up which asks to cancel order or not		
		8. Verify that order number is cancelled and no longer exists in Booked Itinerary page		
TC-120	To Verify Title of every Page reflects what the page objective is. For example Title of Search Hotel page should have "Search Hotel"	1. Launch hotel reservation application using URL as in test data. 2. Login to the application using username and password as in test data. 3. Verify that title of each page is the same as the page objective 4. Click on Search hotel link and verify whether application directs to search hotel form 5. Click on booked itinerary link and verify that application directs to booked itinerary form	http://adactin.com/HotelApp/index.php User:{test username} Password:{test password}	Title of each page should reflect its objective and the buttons should redirect as specified, to the relevant page.

Made in the USA
San Bernardino, CA
30 June 2017